CW01429565

Girls of Color, Sexuality, and Sex Education

Sharon Lamb • Tangela Roberts • Aleksandra Plocha

Girls of Color, Sexuality, and Sex Education

palgrave
macmillan

Sharon Lamb
University of Massachusetts Boston
Boston, Massachusetts, USA

Aleksandra Plocha
University of Massachusetts Boston
Boston, Massachusetts, USA

Tangela Roberts
University of Massachusetts Boston
Boston, Massachusetts, USA

ISBN 978-1-137-60153-7   ISBN 978-1-137-60155-1 (eBook)
DOI 10.1057/978-1-137-60155-1

Library of Congress Control Number: 2016949550

Cover pattern © Harvey Loake

Printed on acid-free paper

This Palgrave Macmillan imprint is published by Springer Nature
The registered company is Nature America Inc.
The registered company address is: 1 New York Plaza, New York, NY 10004, U.S.A.

This book is dedicated to the boys and girls in our Sexual Ethics for a Caring Society classrooms, for their honesty and joy and for their persistent challenges that made us and the curriculum better

ACKNOWLEDGMENTS

The first author would like to thank the Spencer Foundation who provided funding through the New Civics grant program toward the teaching of the curriculum in schools, the Association for Moral Education (AME) for the original grant to write the Sexual Ethics for a Caring Society Curriculum (SECS-C), and University of Massachusetts Boston (UMass Boston) for its incredible support of faculty members' and students' research in growing PhD programs. Lyn Mikel Brown, her former writing partner, still remains a resource, source of encouragement, and guiding light in the area of girls' development.

We would also like to thank the girls, teachers, and counselors at the charter school in a suburb of Boston that supported this work. Their interest in providing a sexual ethics curriculum in addition to a health and prevention curriculum reflected their intensive focus on teaching their students to be responsible citizens and caring partners.

With enormous gratitude we thank Renee Randazzo who was a leader of this project for two years, taught the curriculum for five semesters, wrote first drafts of some portions of Chaps. 4 and 5, and who helped keep the focus on feminist analysis and heteronormativity throughout all our meetings. Her contributions infuse this book at every level. She is an amazing woman who combines her social justice activism in the classroom with an open and caring individualized approach to the students within it.

We also thank Madeline Brodt who taught for one semester and brought her fantastic energy and lively mind to each and every meeting. Lucas Dangler, Kaelin Farmer, and Elena Kosterina were also part of our research group and shaped our thinking with their insights and analysis.

Susan Lambe Sariñana, also a member of the research team, brought us to the wonderful charter school (which prefers to remain unnamed) and introduced us to the lovely counselor there who helped us form the focus groups and to teach our curriculum in the advisory periods.

We especially thank the journal editors and reviewers for the Canadian journal *Girlhood Studies* and the British journal *Gender and Education*. These two journals understand qualitative research and reflexivity required of interpretive work, and support the idea that White researchers as well as researchers of color may write about girls of color with respect and insight.

Finally, we thank our colleagues and peers in the Department of Counseling and School Psychology at UMass Boston, our best resource when we have questions and want to flesh out our thinking. We consider ourselves extremely fortunate to work among them.

CONTENTS

About the Authors

Sharon Lamb, EdD, PhD, ABPP, and Harvard Graduate School of Education graduate, is Professor of Counseling Psychology in the Department of Counseling and School Psychology at UMass Boston. Sharon has written, edited, and coauthored nine books and won two awards: the Books for a Better Life Award, for *Packaging Girlhood*, and the Society for Sex Therapy and Research's book award for *Sex, Therapy, and Kids*. She is a coauthor of the American Psychological Association's *Task Force Report on the Sexualization of Girls* and, with Lyn Mikel Brown and Mark Tappan, *Packaging Boyhood*. Her most recent book, *Sex Ed for Caring Schools: Creating an Ethics-Based Curriculum*, published 2013. She currently cochairs the APA Task Force on the Revision of the Guidelines for Psychological Practice with Girls and Women. Sharon is currently working on the ethical reasoning of bystanders who intervene or choose not to intervene in "sketchy" sexual situations. An experienced clinician, Sharon also sees children, adolescents, adults, and couples at her therapy office in Shelburne, Vermont, and trains students at UMass Boston during their internship year. Sharon also does forensic evaluations in the state of Vermont as an expert on children's development, sexual abuse, harassment, and attachment. Sharon is married to pianist Paul Orgel, has two sons and two grandsons, and lives in Shelburne, Vermont.

Aleksandra Plocha, MS, is a doctoral candidate in the Counseling and School Psychology PhD program at UMass Boston. Aleksandra has her BA in Psychology from Boston College and MS in Mental Health Counseling from the University of Massachusetts Boston. Aleksandra's current research focuses on the topics of resilience, emerging adulthood, and bereavement. Her other areas of research include child and adolescent sexuality, sexual ethics, and familial patterns associated with a child's diagnosis of celiac disease. Aleksandra has experience working with college students, children, adolescents, adults, and families presenting with a variety of concerns, including stress and adjustment difficulties, mood disorders, psychosis, schizophrenia, substance abuse, and complex trauma. She also has experience working with individuals of all ages in psychiatric crisis. She considers her clinical orientation to be eclectic, primarily using client-centered and relational-based therapies.

Tangela Roberts, MS, is a doctoral candidate in the Department of Counseling and School Psychology at UMass Boston. While she is originally from Birmingham, Alabama, she received her MS in Community Counseling from the University of Wisconsin-Madison and her BA from St. John's University in Queens, New York. Primarily, she is interested in intersectionality, social justice, womanism, race and ethnicity, lesbian, gay, bisexual, transgender, and/or queer (LGBTQ) issues, and sexual orientation identity development. Tangela's work on intersectionality research tends to focus on race, ethnicity, sexual orientation, discrimination, and community support. Tangela positions her work to be aimed at developing a better understanding of critical theories, while focusing on intersectional identities, resilience, and support. Previous research projects include the Black identity and community support; impact of biphobia on the sexual orientation identity development process of bisexual identified persons; the role of community support on mental health for bisexual people of color; and African-American and Latino gay family networks and HIV prevention. Tangela has two pet ferrets and lives in Boston, Massachusetts.

CHAPTER 1

Introduction: Girls of Color, Sex, and Healthy Sexuality

Abstract In this introductory chapter, we discuss who are girls of color and how have girls of color and their sexuality been framed in various related fields. We also situate our work in current contexts, briefly reviewing the context of hypersexualization of girls. We introduce the chapters to come and we discuss our positions in terms of our own racial identities and histories with respect to the writing of this book, the interviewing of the girls of color, and the teaching of the sex education classes.

Keywords Girls of color · Pride · Race · Shame · Sexuality · Interesectionality · Hypersexualization · Reflexivity · Feminism · Critique

Who are "girls of color" and why attempt to understand their sexual development apart from White girls? For about a decade, the growth in research and theorizing about sex and sexuality in adolescence has had a primarily White focus; not a purposefully White focus, but a focus that makes assumptions about similarities rather than differences in the way girls of color take in and make meaning about their own sexuality given media messages and discourse about sexuality. Our focus group research with girls of color and our additional research in the classroom teaching the Sexual Ethics for a Caring Society Curriculum (SECS-C) (www.sexandethics.com) to coed classes that included primarily girls of color led us to think differently. We passionately desire to understand

© The Author(s) 2016
S. Lamb et al., *Girls of Color, Sexuality, and Sex Education*,
DOI 10.1057/978-1-137-60155-1_1

how these girls work with cultural discourses about their sexuality and make meaning of their bodies and sexuality in this culture at this time. How might media images and discourse about beauty and sexiness feel different to girls of color? How might historical oppression and lack of visibility contribute to the way they make meaning of the messages they receive and to their own sexual development? What kinds of concerns do they bring to the sex education/sexual ethics classroom? And finally, how do girls of color experience, negotiate, and police the line between sexy-respectful and sexy-slutty, a line all too familiar to developing girls?

In this book, we also broaden the question of what is sexy to examine who "girls of color" are at this point in history in the United States. While there is now a substantial body of research on some specific populations of girls (e.g., Latina, African American, Asian American), the country is changing such that race, ethnicity, and class are no longer neat categories, if ever they actually were. Some schools and neighborhoods are the proverbial melting pots that symbolize democracy in America. In these schools and neighborhood, students may identify as mixed race and/or daughters and sons of African immigrants and thus not how Americans now understand African American identity. They may identify as Caribbean Black, Caribbean Black Latino, or Cuban-American which is different from Puerto Rican or Mexican-American. They may be the daughters and sons of Vietnamese or Cambodian or Laotian immigrants, Chinese-American, Korean-American, Pacific Islanders, Native, or Native American with a number of specific tribal or cultural differences. In the face of such ethnic and racial diversity, typical categories that researchers have students check off on typical demographic forms mask real differences in culture, attitudes, religion, and background.

Class is also a marker of diversity, often assumed to intersect with race but rarely teased out in research. While neighborhoods can sometimes be a way of grouping together individuals of similar socioeconomic class, schools no longer always do this, as Charter schools and traditional public schools pull students from diverse socioeconomic groups, and class is not static.

Sexual orientation is another indicator of diversity, and although so little research exists on girls of color who identify as queer, bi, or lesbian in girlhood or adolescence, we take note that they are doubly marked by sexuality. That is, as a girl of color, particularly a Black girl, she is already read as sexual. As a girl who is not heterosexual, she is defined by her sexual practice. Her sexual risk-taking is more invisible (Riskind et al. 2014) and she may combat this sexualization of her identity by taking a "moral high ground" and labeling other girls "bad girls" and "sluts" to differentiate herself (Payne 2010).

While our own samples are not as diverse as the lists of identities above, given where we were situated in the United States, we set out in this book to both embrace our diverse samples with a qualitative understanding of many differences among the students, while at the same time keeping open the question of how minority status, in all its particularity, may intersect with messages about sex and sexuality in the schools and the world these students live in.

With regard to sex and sexuality, there is precious little psychological research that explores sexual development specifically in girls of color without focusing on risk—pregnancy, sexually transmitted infections (STIs), or abuse. The bulk of the research on girls of color comes from a public health perspective, focusing on findings that some girls of color, Latina and African American, engage in "first sex" earlier than White girls. This research also indicates that they are at greater risk of teen pregnancy (McCree et al. 2003; Wingood et al. 2003). We are thus faced, with a body of research that first and foremost situates girls of color as both oversexed and in danger, in need of services and education for the purposes of prevention. This research examines risk factors such as exposure to rap music videos (Wingood et al. 2003) and depression (Brown et al. 2006), as well as protective factors such as religiosity and the ability to communicate about sex with partners (DiClemente et al. 2001; McCree et al. 2003). This literature positions girls of color as comparatively at greater risk in areas of sexual activity and lends support to the W. E. B. Dubois observation that being Black in America means a girl needs to be constantly aware that others view her as a problem (Harris-Perry 2011).

There is a long racist history of seeing girls of color, particularly African American girls, but also Latina girls, as oversexed or hypersexual. Chapter 2, with its discussion of the research on body image of African American girls and women, will address the relationship of this research to the research on problematic White body ideals and connect this body image research to a history of seeing African American girls as oversexed. Chapter 3 in its discussion of "respect" will address the history of this idea in African American communities of women and its relationship to sexuality. The myth of Black female wantonness has a long history rooted in White justification of the abuse and rape of Black slaves as well as the sexualizing of the exotic and different as a way of preserving an ideal of White purity. This is not only true of Black females but of immigrant women; the earlier social purity movement at the turn of the nineteenth century situated immigrants as the wanton and exotic outsiders that put a supposed White and Protestant purity at risk.

Because of this history, it is dangerous to talk about and research girls of color and sexuality, although it is even more dangerous for girls themselves to be situated in this way. Even in the late twentieth century when poets such as Audre Lorde (1978) wrote so beautifully about owning one's sexuality as sensuality, when Eve Ensler wrote about global violence against women and included the voices of women of color in the Vagina Monologues (Ensler 1998)—in spite of recent criticism for lack of intersectionality (Cooper 2007), when women's studies classes learnt the horror of the "Hottentot Venus," Saartjie Baartman's public degradation (put on display in life and in death for sexual curiosity), and when authors such as Sapphire (1996) and Alice Walker (1992) wrote of the sexual abuse and rape of Black women, there still has been a silence around the healthy sexual development of girls of color.

Girls of color are shaping and expressing their sexuality on a stage for a variety of audiences with a range of expectations. But one of the strongest and most problematic readings of Black sexuality today, in particular, is that of the oversexed Black adolescent girl. While so-called promiscuity in White girls can be read as a result of trauma and while sexual activity of the hook-up culture can be read as a bid for sexual freedom, sexual behavior in the Black teen girl's life is often read as an expression of some innate and animalistic oversexualization. This may not be true for some ethnicities and races but is particularly true for Black girls and thus much of our focus will be on them. We hope not to make other races and ethnicities invisible in this book, and will bring in the diverse voices of our focus groups and classrooms without also trying to make them stand for all minority races. However, our samples, current events, and the existing literature support this closer look at Black girls.

We are cognizant that we are writing at a particularly hopeful and vulnerable time for Black girls. The recent Black Lives Matter (www.black livesmatter.com) movement has drawn attention to the overly punitive, racist, and lethal responses from systems of law and order to experiences of being Black, and Black being interpreted as violent or a problem to be controlled. The "Black Girls Matter" report by Crenshaw et al. (2015) and an essay published in *Diverse Issues in Higher Education* (Cooper 2015) highlight the way lack of protection in school from sexual harassment affects girls, and we might add affects girls' sexual development. It also notes how schools do not identify signs of sexual traumatization nor provide services for Black girls because of this trauma. The report also documents the disproportionate disciplinary action taken against Black girls when they speak out or act out in schools, something noted by our own focus group girls regarding their being punished for the clothes they wear if such clothing appears sexual to teachers and administration even when White girls wear the same clothing. The girls in their report also note the differential treatment of girls who act out from boys who are often positioned as boys just being boys.

We take these crimes against Black girlhood seriously, and acknowledgement of this social injustice pervades this book. While we focus on positive sexual development and girls' strengths, we remember and note the potential underlying hostility in the school environment in which our work was done. In the spirit of intersectionality, a theory that asks us to look at intersecting identities as not merely additive but as constituting a different kind of experience for individuals, we also attend to what it is about Black girls' experience that may be different from the Black boys' experience, whether their sexuality is perceived as more normative and less dangerous than that of Black girls.

This is tricky territory but work that must be done to add to the literature on adolescent sexual development and increase understanding of the context for sexual development of girls of color. We undertake the analysis with some sense of humility, letting the girls' words speak for themselves and giving them voice at times, while at the same time using their words to decode the culture they are negotiating.

We use the words Black and African American differently, at times, in this book. Some of our students identified as Black but not African American. They may have been from Africa, and they may have been Caribbean or South American in background. When citing literature, we will use the identity label the researchers used, typically African American, but when speaking generally about our students and girls, we will attempt to use a more blanket term, Black, to include a variety of girls of color, many of whom have experienced the same reading of their color as hypersexual.

Hypersexualization

Theorists writing on African American women's sexuality suggest a long history of stereotyping African American women as hypersexual when compared to their White counterparts and a history of a belief in the

United States that Black girls in particular need to be controlled (Collins 1990, 2004). These limitations in the expression and experience of sexuality for girls and women of color have a direct relation to the historical view of Black female sexuality as Hottentot Venus and Jezebel, all of whom are considered to be wild and dangerous sexual beings (Henderson 2014; Ross and Coleman 2011; Stephens and Phillips 2003). The hypersexualization of Latinas is described in a similar racialized gender trope, that of being hot-blooded, passionate, teasing, and flirtatious (Jiminez and Abreu 2003).

This hypersexualization has been noted by some as embedded in the hip-hop industries' representation of women, particularly focusing on the images of "gold diggers" and "video vixens" (Stephens and Phillips 2003, 2005; Wallace et al. 2011). The media images presented by mostly male rap artists, where Black women with voluptuous bodies are used as trophies of success, and where, it's been argued, sex sells CDs to a broad, White, male audience, do not help to address the stereotype. While at least one author has seen some Black pop artists as "erotic revolutionaries" (Lee 2010, p. vii), it has been argued that Black women have a stronger and more oppressive stereotype to overcome and that these images do little to help that. Some say the focus on rap and hip-hop alone as exploitative is another racist attempt to undermine Black businesses over White, given the exploitation of women has also been fairly constant in White country or pop music. Girls in our studies have mixed feelings about these pop stars, many of whom are seen as "owning" their sexuality. With regard to Asian American girls, a similar discussion takes place with regard to films. While some filmmakers would argue that stereotyped sexuality of Asian American women opens up the possibility of resistance (Parreñas and Lee 2004), others argue that the stereotypes of Madame Butterflies and always sexually exotic and available is more problematic (Park 2014). We address media images in our research on the focus group girls and their ideas about pop stars and the sexual ethics classroom's discussion of a Lupe Fiasco video, "Bitch Bad."

Stereotypes have consequences. In one study on rape and accountability, individuals tended to demand more accountability for the actions of perpetrators of rape, agree that a rape should be reported, and were more likely to side with the victim when the victim is noted to be White, rather than African American (Jimenez and Abreu 2003). Also, researchers conflating the high risk of inner-city African American adolescent girls with problematic sexuality, focus on negative outcomes and not on strengths

(Stephens and Few 2007; Townsend et al. 2010). Within sex education, girls of color are treated more adult-like (Ferguson 2001) or sexually precocious (Fields 2008; Froyum 2010; Pascoe 2007). And for Latinas, the hypersexualization myth has also been noted to influence sex education classrooms through relentless emphasizing that girls can get pregnant and that early pregnancy is consistent with Latina culture (Garcia 2009).

When the American Psychological Association's Task Force Report on the Sexualization of Girls (2007) was published, there was some concern on the part of the authors that the research on the effects of music focused inordinately on rap, even though one study showed that rap music had more sexually degrading lyrics and that those children who listened to music containing objectifying and limiting characterizations of sexuality had earlier sex (Martino et al 2006). Critics of the report and the literature in it pointed out that the voices of girls of color seemed not to be included (Gill 2012; Ringrose and Renold 2012) or that the research reproduced stereotypes of childhood innocence that are racialized and buy into a White purity myth (Egan and Hawkes 2008).

While the media may represent girls of color as hypersexualized, thus influencing how Whites may view girls of color, girls of color may see White girls in a similar vein. As the idea of "respect" has been advanced in Black families and religious and political ideals of respectability promoted, an idea we develop in Chap. 3, sometimes, White girls, and particularly in this era of hook-ups and casual sex, are set up as poor examples of developing sexuality. Weekes (2002), in the UK, studied the discourse of 29 Afro-Caribbean teen girls which showed Black girls "othering" White girls as hypersexualized and deviant, thus positioning themselves as respectable and purer even when they do not see themselves as passive with regard to sex. Espiritu's (2001) analysis of the "otherness" of White people to Filipino immigrants shows how Filipino families teach their children that White families care less for their children and let them do whatever they want, resulting in White promiscuity compared to the virtuousness of Filipina girls.

AIMS OF THIS BOOK

In our book, we attempt to consider girls in all their diversity. We consider them as girls and not women, that is, as still developing, learning, and changing. We are careful not to position girls as all-knowing, with gems of understanding that only savvy researchers can draw out or bring to light. The positioning of girls in such a way, common to some of the "voice" research of the 1980s and 1990s, both idealizes and misrepresents girls. We take a both/and perspective. While they are certainly smart, active participants in the research we present, and we consider their views and beliefs in a full way, they are also less knowledgeable about some subjects (e.g., feminism), more influenceable, and still developing. Moreover, given some of our work in classrooms was "consciousness raising" work, representing the girls as always and only fully representing themselves, their true beliefs, their authentic feelings, and not the culture in which they live, would be a grave mistake. We don't make a sharp divide between what is authentic feeling and what is a reproduction of cultural ideology and can't. But we do try to figure out how, when a girl expresses a cultural belief as her own honest thinking, she makes this belief work for her as she is situated among other teens, in a school, in a family, and in the United States.

We researchers, as focus group leaders, classroom teachers, and research group participants, are also a part of the culture and don't set ourselves above it. Because of this, we felt it was our obligation to challenge our beliefs and attitudes, our interpretations, and our in-the-moment responses to the girls. In the analyses that follow, we attempt to call out times in which our own ideologies as well as cultural, ethnic, and racial backgrounds may have been influencing the interactions, that is, taking a reflexive approach (Henwood 2008). A reflexive approach attends to our individual psychologies, cultural influences, the dynamics of the classrooms, and the social embeddedness of leading the focus groups and delivering lessons from the SECS-C curriculum.

Theorists have expressed concerns that, when qualitative researchers represent the marginalized others' voices and experiences without reflexivity, they may produce a "colonizing discourse of the other," speaking for others while "occluding themselves and their own investments" (Henwood 2008, p. 49). To address this concern, reflexive researchers are called upon to reveal their identities and make themselves vulnerable. As older (than the students), feminist-identified female teachers, all but one of whom was White, our own histories of oppression and privileges (in relation to the students and as perceived by students) affected the dynamics of the SECS-C classrooms. While Whiteness of all but one of the teachers was salient, there were other commonalities including experiences with sexual harassment, abuse, and assault as well as connections to immigration and to working class and low-income familial environments.

We are as follows, one White Jewish 60-year-old professor who grew up in a low-income household that transformed to a middle-class household by the time she graduated high school. Her parents were uneducated and she was the only sibling who received a college education. Her relationship to communities of color began with bussing in 5th grade and the lessons on "integration" that followed in her junior high school. To this day she feels ashamed that she declined an invitation to sleep over at a Black friend's home, because she was fearful of the girl's brothers and some vague notion of Black men's sexuality. This fear did change during high school. In her very diverse high school, one known at the time to represent the exact racial percentages of the United States, she was the only White student who took the African American history course, her heart pounding when the teacher went around the room and asked each student what African American leader they most admired. Should she name Martin Luther King and say the obvious? Or would that betray her ignorance that that was the only name that came to mind. Today she regularly discusses race with one of her best friends, Beverly Colston, the director of ALANA services at the University of Vermont. Her extended family now includes biracial nieces, as well as family members who are still low-income rather than middle-class.

A 28-year-old Black female doctoral student grew up in a poverty-class household within Birmingham, Alabama. Raised by her mother, she and her older brother both eventually went on to attend PhD programs in different disciplines. As a child living in a city known to be an early spotlight of American race relations, the concepts of racial identity and social perceptions of Black people and cultures was ingrained in her interactions with peers, family, and her community at large. As a child who also was raised in the south, she became acutely aware of the impression that respectability politics leaves on the psyche of a young African American woman. The community of Black women who aided in her upbringing (including her mother, her grandmother, aunts, and church members), employed and reinforced many aspects of respectability politics as a way to derive a sense of dignity when living in places where the color of their skin deemed them to be undignified. She often notes that she doesn't remember a moment in which she became aware of her race; rather she became aware of others' assumptions and biases about her race when she left Birmingham to attend universities in ethnically diverse Queens, New York and majority White in Madison, Wisconsin and Boston, Massachusetts. Growing up in a city with a long history of racial justice and civil rights has fostered her own commitment to social justice. This is translated in her advocacy and activism for racial and gender justice. Tangela's research, teaching, and clinical interests align with intersectionality, social justice, womanism, identity and community among LGBTQ people of color, and racial justice activism.

The third author is a 30-year-old White female doctoral student who grew up in the suburbs of Philadelphia. Ali's mother is a PhD Historian whose research focused on the experiences of immigrant minority groups in the United States. Ali thanks her mother for instilling in her a strong pride in her Polish heritage, as well as an interest in and appreciation for different cultures. This fueled Ali to visit and live in numerous countries as a student and tourist. She has worked with volunteers on a Navajo reservation in New Mexico who were addressing the abandonment of children born with fetal alcohol syndrome. In Marrakesh, Morocco, she learned her worth in camels when an older gentleman offered to buy her from the male friend with whom she was traveling. And in a rural town in Nicaragua, she was inspired by the strength of young teenage mothers who sought prenatal care. These and many other experiences have fostered Ali's interest in exploring race, culture, and privilege, and have led Ali to adopt a framework in her research and clinical work that considers these and other sociopolitical factors. Ali's fellow members of her PhD cohort—who are among her very best friends—are a racially and ethnically diverse group. Their conversations in the classroom, the PhD lounge, and over drinks continually include discussions of how race and cultural background influence one's worldviews and lived experiences.

The focus group leaders included the first and third author, a mixed-race (Asian American and White) woman who was working as an intern in the counseling office at the Charter school, and two other women who identified as White. Among the group were women who identified as queer.

The teachers of the seven classes were the three authors of the book, and two additional White women in their 30s, Renee Randazzo and Madeline Brodt. The researchers, focus group leaders, and curriculum teachers were of varying sexual orientations and came from both middle and working class backgrounds.

Within the research group – that sometimes included a gay mixed-race man – we teachers reflected on our own histories, including privilege, histories of oppression, race, and class and we explored to what extent these factors interacted with students' histories and expectations as well as our own. White teachers could check in with the one African American teacher (second author) after the class to see if the discussion in her class differed. When the discussion differed, we would consider in what ways race played a part. There might have been an assumption that her class would be different because students outwardly initially expressed enthusiasm for having the African American teacher for their section of the class. As noted earlier, the democratic classroom was emphasized and an introductory lesson had students come up with a plan for how discussions would be run and how disruptions would be handled. Students could opt out of the course or any particular class and were treated as willing participants encouraged to speak their minds.

With regard to the feminist theory that informs this work, we do not believe in any essentialist view of gender or race, but see both as intersecting and expressions of intersections of meaning within a culture. We see labels such as "girl" or "White" as positioning people in social hierarchies. The idea that girls are "socialized" to act or think in a certain way is not as appealing to us as the idea that girls are situated in experience in such a way so that certain meanings of who they are and what their acts mean become more or less salient or available to them to use when figuring out the world around them.

We also take seriously the tradition of "womanist" feminism, a feminism that includes an intense identification with female-centered experience and that looks for and brings to light those experiences and stories of strength and determination in the midst of adversity. While we are unlike womanist scholars who use standpoint theory, taking at face value the lived experiences of Black women, we do not dismiss experience or the words of our participants as merely discourse, but look to the fuller meaning of their experience and their words in the historical and immediate contexts in which they're expressed. To this extent we are both womanist, attending to moments of strength and resistance, as well as Discourse Analytic, interpreting their expressions with an attention to context which includes history and an in-depth look at dominant and complicated institutions such as the media.

Within our feminism it is important to define what a positive sexuality might look like in light of the historical and modern obstacles we present. Sexuality, within liberal and progressive discourse, has long been a marker of freedom. The ability to walk freely on the streets at night without fear of rape, to express one's sexuality without fear of judgment, and to seek out sexual pleasure in meaningful ways are all connected to freedom. In today's world, in the United States, the phrase sexual freedom can mean the freedom to hook-up with whomever one wants. The phrase has been used to combat repercussions of what today is called "slut-shaming." But sexual freedom is like all freedoms and involves for girls, as Fine and McClelland (2006) have argued, institutional supports for that freedom such as sex education and access to contraception, and as Tolman (2012) has argued, an opportunity to understand their bodies' expressions of sexual pleasure. Bay-Cheng (2012) explains that sexual freedom also comes from access to feminist rather than self-blaming discourses about why one has run into trouble with one's sexuality. Ward (2004) hopes that Black youths will be exposed to a pop culture that is less commodifying and still sexually expressive. And Lamb (2002, 2006) has argued that healthy sexuality develops early in girlhood with permission to play sexually and talk about sexuality without repercussions.

*   *   *

The following chapter on body image reviews the existing literature that, for the most part, celebrates Black girls' less restrictive body ideals in US culture and continues to render invisible the bodies of a multitude of other races and ethnicities as if bodies express either Black or White aesthetics. But as we add in the voices of the girls we interviewed, it will be clear that that which appears less restrictive from a White perspective may have its own restrictions or come with its own judgments within the Black or Latina community. In this chapter, we also examine the sexualization literature that looks at the influence of media on girls' desires surrounding becoming a sexual person. In the chapter on respect, Chap. 3, we explore the ways in which these discourses intersect with girls' wishes to be sexy and sexual, differentiating these two. We look at the history of the idea of respect in the Black community in the United States as well as the discourse around pride, and explore how these concepts may both police and protect girls from damaging stereotypes about girls of color's sexuality. We bring in data from our focus groups and sex education research to show how this discourse is also used to police the borders around girls' acceptable behavior in adolescence and can interfere with girlhood solidarity. In Chap. 4, we look more in depth at the vulnerabilities girls face in the sex education classroom by seeing how these discourses of hypersexuality, respect, and pride come into play in discussions about objectification, coercion, and positive sexuality. In Chap. 5, we look at how the literature on media influence the sexuality of girls of color and examine classroom discussion of the Lupe Fiasco video, "Bitch Bad," which was part of one of the SECS-C lessons. And in Chap. 6, we propose several ways in which communities, educators, agencies, and counselors can respond to the needs of girls of color for sex education and positive messaging about sexuality. We address media sexualization, sex education, and support within schools and families, based on girls' hopes for a more sex positive developmental atmosphere that honors who they are and who they can become at this time in this country.

CHAPTER 2

Body Image, Sexy, and Sexualization

Abstract The chapter on body image begins with a review of the literature on the White "thin body ideal" and the work that shows that Black
and Latina girls have been shown to have different beauty standards. These
latter ideals have been described as more permissive in terms of body size
and shape. We explore the various reasons this might be true and
describe research that shows that exposure to predominantly White thin
ideal media has less of an effect on girls of color. We also discuss the idea
that while the body ideals might be different, the idea that they are more
"permissive" reflects a White and privileged perspective. We use our focus
group discussions to show that there may also be restrictions and shaming
in communities of girls of color when a girl does not attain an ideal, even if
it is not the thin one. We also explore the way girls understand that fuller
figures make them vulnerable and more prone to being seen as sexual and
hypersexual by teachers and other adults in their school. We also draw on
discourse studies from outside of the United States in which researchers
attempted to understand the complexity of what sexiness is with regard to
the intersection of race, sex, and sexuality.

Keywords Body image · Sexualization · Body acceptance · Beauty ·
Colorism · Standards

© The Author(s) 2016   15
S. Lamb et al., *Girls of Color, Sexuality, and Sex Education*,
DOI 10.1057/978-1-137-60155-1_2

When we consider the research that exists on body image and sexualization among girls of color, there are two main—and conflicting—themes: that African American perceptions of the female body serve as a protective factor for girls of color against harmful media beauty stereotypes (e.g., Alleyne and LaPoint 2004; Boyd et al. 2011; Hesse-Biber et al. 2004) and that there are dangers associated with girls of color being sexual too soon, including earlier sexual debut (e.g., Fletcher et al. 2015) and higher incidence of sexually transmitted diseases (STDs) (McCree et al. 2003). In this chapter, we focus on the former collection of research and discuss factors that influence body and self-image among girls of color. As there is so little research on body image of girls of color who are not Black, we focus on Black girls and attempt to add these other studies in whenever possible.

Body Acceptance and a More Realistic Ideal

How exactly can the idea of "the African American body" be a protective factor for girls of color? For over a decade, an argument around this has been that the "big is beautiful" message that is associated with African American bodies shields girls from the media messages that present White, stick-thin models as an ideal of beauty and sexuality (Alleyne and LaPoint 2004). African American women consider an ideal sexy body to be "thick" and "curvaceous, with large hips, a rounded backside, and ample thighs" (Hesse-Biber et al. 2004, p. 55). And, African American adolescents endorse fuller personal body ideals than their White and Latina peers (Gordon et al. 2010; Kelch-Oliver and Ancis, 2011; Viladrich et al. 2009), are more satisfied with their weight, and less likely to see themselves as overweight even when they are, according to medical standards (Boyd et al. 2011). Some research suggests that Black women may consider their bodies to be fixed entities that were God-given or biologically endowed (Hesse-Biber et al. 2004). Belief in God, body acceptance, and appreciation for features that are considered "average" all help adolescent girls of color maintain a positive body image (Pope et al. 2014).

Indeed, size and weight may not be as big of a deal when it comes to body image for Black girls as it is for their White peers. Adolescent girls of color have been shown to be less preoccupied with their size and weight than White adolescents (Hesse-Biber et al. 2004; Fitzsimmons-Craft and Bardone-Cone 2012; Warren 2014) and less likely to judge themselves according to their weight (Hesse-Biber et al. 2004). Issues like body surveillance and body dissatisfaction have also been shown to be greater concerns among Caucasian women than among African American women (Fitzsimmons-Craft and Bardone-Cone 2012). African American adolescent girls tend to have less rigid concepts of their ideal body type, have more favorable body image evaluations (Fitzsimmons-Craft and Bardone-Cone 2012; Roberts et al. 2006), and be more realistic when it comes to accepting their body size (Demarest and Allen 2000; Duke 2000). In a study of how ethnicity and acculturation impact body attitudes and eating disorders, a group of researchers found that African-descended women reported the most positive body attitudes and the lowest risk of eating disorders among all groups studied (including European- and Asian-descended women) (Sussman et al. 2007). And, among women who are medically overweight and obese, Black women report lower perceived weight and higher self-evaluations of attractiveness than White obese and overweight women (Chithambo and Huey 2013).

For Asian American women, it may be the opposite. The thin ideal appears to be alive and well according to research. Asian American girls report the most body dissatisfaction across large samples of diverse teens (Bucchianeri et al. 2016). Acculturation seems to be a mediator of this dissatisfaction as well, correlating with enhanced risk of eating disorders (Xie et al. 2010).

With regard to Latina women, one study of Mexican American women shows that comparing oneself to other women is more likely than media consumption to cause body image dissatisfaction, and that acculturation has a complex relationship to body image. In general, strong ethnic identity predicts lower levels of body dissatisfaction on most appearance areas, among White, Black, and Latina women. Mexican American women who have internalized White ideals but have trouble accepting their ethnic identity, on the other hand, experience the most stress regarding body image.

BODY IMAGE AND THE MEDIA

Media is a powerful and increasingly ever-present force in our society that both threatens and supports positive body image in girls. Research supports the fact that media has a significant impact on how both White adolescents and adolescent girls of color view their bodies (e.g., Botta 2003; Brown et al. 2006; Greenwood and Dal Cin 2012). Furthermore, regardless of race, idealization of media images has been correlated with adolescents' desire to be thin and the tendency to experience dissatisfaction with their body. That being said, the type of media that African

American adolescents are exposed to likely contributes to their more positive body image and realistic ideals (Botta 2003; Brown et al. 2006; Greenwood and Dal Cin 2012; Schooler et al. 2004). Also, while they are consuming the same amount of media, adolescent girls of color may not be as influenced by it as White girls and may not internalize what they see into their self-concept and self-perception. One study found, for example, that the sexual behavior of friends and parental expectations were more influential than the media (Brown et al. 2006). Another study yielded similar results among a sample of Hispanic adolescent girls (Ferguson et al. 2014). In this study, the authors found that television exposure to "thin ideal media" did not negatively impact girls' body dissatisfaction or eating disorder symptoms. Peer competition, however—which was perpetuated by the use of social media—brought about these negative outcomes.

One reason that Black girls may not be as influenced by media images is the fact that most of the problem images are of White women, and thus are not women that these girls could or would hope to emulate (e.g., Duke 2000; Schooler et al. 2004). They may also simply not be interested in media that is not geared toward them. For example, one researcher found that African American 12- to 18-year olds were not interested, and subsequently not influenced by the content of mainstream beauty magazines, because they did not believe the advice in these magazines was aimed at them (Duke 2000). There is similar research related to Latina women, who are also underrepresented in popular media (Murnen and Don 2012). Other research suggests that adolescent girls of color may be more skeptical consumers of media than their White peers, and that distrust of images presented in the media can serve to protect body-related attitudes and behaviors (Pope et al. 2014).

This does not seem to be as true for Asian American young women, even though stars like Lucy Liu are gaining prominence and comedians like Mindy Kaling bring to light issues regarding weight and body image on TV and in comedy routines. Some researchers believe that because Asian American girls and women are so rarely represented in the media, they are more likely to internalize the thin ideal of White women (Javier and Belgrave 2015). On the other hand, Pacific Islander women, who tend to have higher body weight and who are also underrepresented in the media, also tend to be more satisfied with their appearance than Asians and Whites (Latner et al. 2011).

When girls of color do view women in the media who more closely mirror their skin color, the results seem to be positive. One study revealed a connection among a sample of African American women who were exposed to African American models and more positive self-esteem and body image (Frisby 2004). Similarly, in their sample of 17- to 22-year-old women, another researcher found that those who watched Black-oriented television reported healthier body image compared to those who watched mainstream television that was not geared toward Black viewers (Schooler et al. 2004). The authors also showed that for the women in this latter category, watching mainstream television had no impact on their body image.

Despite these positive findings, it is important to note that girls and women of color are by no means immune to the negative impact that media can have on body image. Black women still feel pressure to be thin, pressure to conform to the beauty preferences of men, and competition with other Black women to be beautiful (Poran 2006). They also do internalize idealized media images which negatively impacts their body esteem and their satisfaction with their appearance (Capodilupo 2015). However, as we will discuss next in more depth, the images that Black women internalize are not only related to body image, but also to culturally relevant beauty ideals, such as lighter skin and long, straight hair.

BODY IMAGE AND SKIN COLOR

When it comes to discussing body image among girls of color, it's not all about body shape and size. Skin color is also a very important part of this discussion. The term *colorism* refers to the preference and desire for light skin and the features that accompany light skin, such as hair texture, broadness of nose, eye color, and fullness of lips (Thompson and Keith 2001). Colorism (Walker 1983) is rooted in systematic racism that has linked lighter skin with higher status historically held by Europeans (Hunter 2002).

Research shows that socially constructed notions about race and gender impact how women of color perceive themselves (Awad et al. 2015; Hunter 2002). Among African American women of color, a lighter complexion has been positively correlated with self-esteem and feelings of perceived mastery (Thompson and Keith 2001, 2004), as well as evaluations of self-worth and attractiveness (Awad et al. 2015; Falconer and Neville 2000; Hill 2002). Interestingly, the association between skin tone and attractiveness is weaker among men of color, and is consistent with other research showing that fair skin tone is considered to be a feminine characteristic among African Americans (Hill 2002). How satisfied an African American woman is with her skin color has also been shown to be connected to how she evaluates other dimensions of body image, including her overall appearance and satisfaction with specific body areas (Falconer and Neville 2000). Other research highlights the fact that within group, skin-color stratification also impacts self-evaluation of body image (Awad et al. 2015). Unlike other physical characteristics associated with beauty (e.g., hair), skin tone is far more difficult to manipulate. Thus, skin tone is an influential element associated with body image among Black women because there are evaluations made by both in-group and out-group members.

BODY IMAGE AND OTHER BEAUTY STANDARDS

Beauty expectations for Black women are also important, and include not only skin color but also hair and facial features (e.g., Capodilupo and Kim 2014). Their self-perceptions are often influenced by Black men, who on the one hand may accept a fuller figure than society in general, but on the other hand show simultaneous preference for Eurocentric features, including long, straight hair and a lighter skin tone (Capodilupo and Kim 2014). Very interestingly, Latina and White women report greater dissatisfaction with their facial features than Black women (Warren 2014). So, while women of color evaluate themselves according to these features, they may ultimately be more accepting of them than their White peers. And, positively evaluating these features has benefits for adolescent girls' self-esteem, and in turn, their behavior. Afrocentric image may be related to sex. Dark versus light skin, full lips, and nose compared to thick lips and narrow nose, and dark, curly, and course hair versus straight, fine hair are features traditionally associated with an Afrocentric image (Plybon et al. 2009), and girls who positively evaluate these features seem better able to feel effective in sexual situations where their assertiveness is important.

THE BLACK BODY AND HYPERSEXUALIZATION

A consideration of body image among girls of color would not be complete without a discussion of the Black female body itself, and specifically, how it is and has been viewed by society. Historically, the bodies of Black females have been considered animalistic, unnatural, and even grotesque (Carroll 2000). Specific parts of the Black female body have been the subject of gross fascination and scrutiny, including the buttocks, thighs, and breasts (Mowatt et al. 2013). A disturbing example of this is the story of Sara Baartman, a woman from South Africa who was enslaved during the 1800s. During her enslavement, a British doctor wrote about her body shape and specific parts, discussing her breasts, genitalia, and large buttocks as "amusing, inferior, and oversexed" (Mowatt et al. 2013, p. 649). As a result of this report, Baartman was placed on display, and individuals could pay to view her naked body. When she passed away, her body parts were preserved and publically displayed until 1974.

While we would be outraged at such inhumane treatment of a woman's body today, the truth is that the Black female body is still very much on display and our society still has a fascination with Black women's large butts and ample breasts. Take a look at rap or hip-hop music videos or pornography with Black women, and you'll see these body parts on full display and fetishized (Miller-Young 2010; Mowatt et al. 2013). Black female athletes receive similar treatment—for example, the media's focus on pro tennis star Serena Williams' large and muscular butt. Williams has ranked Number 1 in the world for singles tennis on six different occasions, but the media can't get over talking about her butt.

Because of these body features, Black women have historically been stereotyped as hypersexual, animalistic, manipulative, and promiscuous, and as always looking for and wanting sex (Collins 2004; Mowatt et al. 2013). This is referred to as the "Jezebel" image of Black women, and it has been used to justify White men's exploitation and rape of Black women. The idea was that if Black women are always ready for sex and seeking it out, White men are not taking advantage of them, harassing them, or raping them, but rather responding to their solicitations. Thus, the Black body became synonymous with hypersexualization and the perception that Black women are promiscuous (Harris-Perry 2011; Miller-Young 2010; Mowat et al. 2013). Once again, we can see this in such media as music videos and pornography. That being said, these stereotypes are not limited to those in the media spotlight, but rather are pervasive among all Black women. When Black women exhibit what we would consider very normal expressions of their sensuality or sexuality—including wearing revealing clothing or showing public physical affection to a partner—it can be interpreted as confirming the stereotype that Black women are indeed hypersexualized and promiscuous (Harris-Perry 2011). The implication of this is that Black women are often stereotyped and receive unwanted attention simply because of the body they've been born with.

SEXUALIZATION AND BODY IMAGE: FOCUS GROUP DISCUSSIONS

We spoke to girls about body image in our focus groups and some of this analysis appears in our published papers (Lamb et al. 2016; Lamb and Plocha 2015). Here we highlight aspects of the discussion that couldn't be elaborated on in shorter publications. As noted in the introduction, we created three focus groups with girls of color who attended the same school in the Boston suburbs. The focus groups were organized by age: 8th–9th graders, 10th–11th graders, and 11th–12th graders. Out of 17 girls, 12 identified as African American or Black, two as Latina, two as multiracial, and one as Native American. Each focus group was led by graduate students and/or a professor, all except one of whom were White.

We asked the girls questions about their perceptions of what it means to be sexy, what they believe constitutes being sexy, and what teenage girls in general might think it means to be sexy. The girls were also asked to reflect on how these conceptualizations of sexiness might differ according to race and ethnicity, as well as how media might influence their opinions.

Differences Between the Black and White Body Ideal

The girls in our focus group jumped right into the narrative of pride in the Black body and most strongly supported the "big is beautiful" message regarding Black female bodies even when they themselves did not identify as Black. In one conversation the girls discussed how other racial groups envy Black bodily features and hint at some appropriation. One girl complained, "They're praising people on, like, attributes that Black people have had for generations. Like 'Oh, Jennifer Lopez' butt'. Well yeah, that's nothing special if she was a Black girl." The girls were alert to contradictions like when girls who are not Black celebrate the Black body while simultaneously valuing a lighter skin color: "Some people who don't have that shape that Black people do, they try to do that. But yet then we try to have lighter skin to look Latina." In pointing this out, perhaps the girls were trying to express that body, skin color, and attitude together, can't be compartmentalized and then commodified for other girls to adopt.

Girls also saw this praise for the Black body as progress for Black girls and also as showing a kind of superiority over White girls. One girl shared, "But now I think it evolved to like thick and big. 'Cause I know a lot of people are looking at the big girls, and the, the thick girls are sexy too." And, "For White girls, it's like still 5 years ago for them because I never really hear about the big white girls being famous. . . I always hear about the White girls, the size 2. But Black girls, like, we have big people to also look forward, to look up to."

One of the African American girls in the group described the regulatory way "big is beautiful" can play out in the Black community:

> I feel uncomfortable, because I feel like sexy to me is like you need to have like, boobs and butt, and . . . I, like my family, my whole family has that kind of body, and they make me feel like, not the black sheep per se', but, "I came out differently."

Another who championed celebrities of color who have curvy figures and criticized others who lost weight in an effort to conform to the White thin-body ideal shared, "I look up to [Kimora Lee Simmons] 'cause she's like, she's sort of a big girl. But she knows how to work what she has; it's like, ok, whatever." When the discussion turned to Jennifer Hudson, though, an actress and singer who has been a spokesperson for Weight Watchers, the girls seemed to take pause. Some saw Hudson as another celebrity who was comfortable with her fuller figure but "forced" to lose weight because of the industry. Another girl ventured to say that she thought Hudson looked good post-weight-loss. It may have been that the White interviewers presented a context in which the girls of color felt a need to assert pride in Blackness, making it harder to assert when one preferred the thin ideal. It could also have been that bringing girls of color together to talk about sexiness is tricky territory and that the group had to establish a "Black is beautiful" and "Big is beautiful" consensus before introducing other ideas that might contradict this.

Skin Color

One area in which the girls in the focus groups eagerly pursued discussion was skin color. The girls shared the pride they associated with being Black, and simultaneously discussed the benefits associated with having lighter skin. The girls clearly saw the cultural value placed on having lighter skin as well as the benefits of being seen as more attractive and sexually desirable. They shared that girls with darker skin have to work harder to be sexy and compensate for their darker skin color by having "the best body ever." One girl shared, "Like if you're dark skinned, if you don't have that hair, they don't want you. If you don't have that butt, they don't want it. If you don't have that chest, they don't want it."

Savvy about factors that influenced these perceptions, one girl stated, "I think media plays a big role. Especially in rap songs, hip-hop music, where they always have in their video, they have the light skinned girls." Another girl told the others she had read an article in which rapper Lil' Wayne told one of his "groupie girls" that she was "really pretty to be a dark skinned girl." What was interesting was this same girl agreed with Lil' Wayne's assertion, saying aloud that "dark skinned girls are not that beautiful," adding, "if guys see a light skinned girl, they're just like, 'Yeah, I want her'." In this moment, it appeared not merely as if she believed that dark skinned girls were not that beautiful, but that she believed it because the culture and particularly men believe that.

The girls also related stories about family messages about skin color. One girl of Haitian background stated:

> I've kind of been trained to think that light skin is better … In Haiti, honestly, if you are light skin, you automatically, you … they automatically think that you're gonna make it better in life, like you're gonna be … that you're gonna be that big person. But if you're dark, then you're like in the corner or whatever.

One girl described her family as "extremely light skinned," and went on to say that many members will still "only marry people who are lighter than them, because they're still into this, like mentality that they have to whiten their race." If we think about these discussions as ways in which girls can "other" an unpopular idea, Haitian families, family members, (but not them) have this unpopular view, another girl brought it closer to home. She stated that she knows girls "who are darker skinned … they'll be like, 'Oh, I'm not going to marry or have a kid with a darker skin, I want my kid to be pretty'."

While the girls agreed about the benefits of having light skin, they varied in terms of how they felt about this. As noted above, some *othered* the idea (e.g., *they* might believe this but I don't) or challenged the idea by judging those who do. A couple of girls talked about themselves. They expressed self-doubt about—and even guilt for—their beliefs. But they put these beliefs in a developmental perspective, indicating they would grow out of it. One girl explained:

> And the messed up thing about it is that I'm not even attracted to White guys, I'm attracted to Black guys, and I'm willing to say, "Oh yeah, that

White guy is sexy," just 'cause I want my child to like, to come out lighter or whatever, but...yeah. But I'm maturing with that.

Achieving Sexiness is Harder for Black Girls

The idea of having to compensate emerged not only in relation to dark skin but in simply being Black. Girls in the focus group received the message that Black girls have to work harder and put forth more effort to be sexy than do White girls. The girls often agreed with each other that looking sexy requires more time, energy, and money. One participant explained, "I feel like Black people, we have to do a lot to look sexy." Another group member added:

> Most white girls that I hang out with like their like version of sexy isn't like, they're not going to wear, like, um, some skintight jeans or something like that. Like they're probably gonna wear, like they're gonna wear short shorts, like with a sweater, and then they're just sexy because they have a messy bun on the top of their head.

Again, this conversation seemed to contradict the notion that the Black body—which is fuller and consequently inherently sexy—is a source of pride. The girls discussed the kind of money that was needed to look sexy and noted that they see around them and the media more and more rich Black people. In this way, looking sexy has become equated with being rich and thus positions the sexy body as the commodified body.

Punishment for Being Sexy

The girls also talked about how they and other girls have been punished for being sexy which included negative comments from peers, "nasty" remarks from boys, and even assaults. The girls contrasted these consequences with their perceived experience of White girls, for whom they saw sexy as unproblematic. Note that when the following girl speaks, she begins with an apology, perhaps with a nod to the interviewers:

> Not to sound racist, but white girls can get away with little different things. Like at public schools there's like not a dress code, but there's some like, a certain extent here you can't wear certain things. And my friend had told

me about what White girls are wearing really really really really short shorts, and they had one short shorts with one of theirs and they got sent home. And I just felt like that was not okay. I think it was 'cause they were skinnier. But same at this school. Like if you're skinnier and you wear skinny pants, you can get in, but if you're thick and you have like thick thighs and you wear skinny jeans or whatever here, you get kicked out.

Here she highlights the predicament that it is dangerous to look *naturally* sexy, that the Black body, naturalized as thicker and more voluptuous, is likely to be read as *intentionally and provocatively* sexy. Lola echoes this sentiment, commenting, "You get busted easily... Like it's 'cause you have a shape." The girls appear to struggle considerably with this double standard and with the idea of being punished for having a body that in other areas of their lives they have been taught to celebrate. Becky attempts to explain this occurrence by making the issue not about girl's bodies, but about what boys want. She states, "I think that [my teacher] thinks that when you're bigger like you, say you have thick thighs, boys will want to look and if you're skinny, there's nothing to look at." Becky is not able to stay with this position for long, however, ultimately declaring, "It's not really fair 'cause if you're wearing the same thing and one's gonna get kicked out and one's not? That's not even right."

So the solution to this kind of reading of the Black body is that girls cover up their bodies to avoid negative attention from peers, boys, and teachers: "And I do not want to be treated that way, so I purposely wear as much clothes as possible. Like I'm the person who wears sweaters in the summer, because I don't like to be talked about like that. That is completely disgusting to me." Another girl shared how covering up is a matter of safety, stating, "I try my hardest to cover my body, 'cause like me covering my body is still getting people following me... So I don't want to get killed for wearing jeans." This girl actually suggested that girls get killed for looking sexy which makes her cautious about how she dresses. From "Black and Big is Beautiful" to "don't wear your sexy jeans or you might get killed," we can see the problems with being visible (which we will discuss further in the following chapter on Respect). We also see the perceived double standard that exists for Black and White girls, in that Black girls get "called out" for being sexy—without even trying—because their bodies differ from the culturally preferred thin White ideal, and because of cultural stereotypes about Black girls and sex (e.g., Collins 2004).

CHAPTER 3

Respect

Abstract The idea of respect has a long history in the Black community and has come to mean many things. We begin by looking at the history of the Black church and Christian women's entreaties to other women in the Black community to conduct themselves with respect. This was an effort to counteract stereotypes of Black female promiscuity. A highly contested topic in Black Studies today, the "politics of respectability" has also been seen as a way that Black, middle class families could differentiate themselves from low income Black families during the 1930s when more Black individuals were getting college educations and becoming part of the professional class. We suggest that these messages about respect may also work to support a negative attitude about developing sexuality that girls need to work around. How are they to become sexual in respectful ways in an era of enormous exposure to a variety of sexual practices? We review their focus group discussion about girls who go "too far" or are "too sexy" and their condemnation of them as not respecting themselves.

Keywords Respect · Racism · Discourse · Religion · Dignity · Family values · Patriarchy · Virgin/whore dichotomy · Exotification · Politics

This chapter focuses on the idea of respect, which has a long history in the Black community and has come to mean many things to a variety of marginalized groups. Although the idea of "respect" and "respectable behavior" may be a way of shaping and policing girls' behavior in Asian American, Latina, and

© The Author(s) 2016   27
S. Lamb et al., *Girls of Color, Sexuality, and Sex Education*,
DOI 10.1057/978-1-137-60155-1_3

Native families, it has particular meaning in the Black community. We begin by looking at the history of the Black women's community efforts to establish social clubs in order to highlight Black women as respectable and counteract stereotypes of Black female promiscuity (Higginbotham 1992). A highly contested topic in Black Studies today (Harris 2003, 2014; Kennedy 2015), the "politics of respectability" can also be understood within a historical context. For example, during the 1930's more Black individuals were obtaining college education and gaining access into the professional class. This increased the Black middle class and led to the use of "the politics of respectability" as a way to differentiate from Black poverty class families. Today, however, theorists point out that the idea of respectability derives from an "ideology of middle-class morality that is intimately linked to White nationalism in Europe and the United States" (Duncan 2005, p. 4).

Within this history, there exists an understanding of mother/daughter relationships. In these relationships mothers were concerned that their daughters' free expression would increase their vulnerabilities, leading to negative perceptions of others, including damaging opinions and racist interpretations of these free expressions (Collins 2000). Collins (2000) emphasizes, however, that for many Black girls, models of womanhood included displays of independence, self-confidence, and self-reliance far earlier than the 1960s (Collins 2000).

This social history also includes a prevalent concern that these messages about respect and pride may work to support a negative attitude about developing sexuality that girls need to work around. How are they to become sexual in respectful ways in an era of enormous exposure to a variety of sexual practices? We review focus group discussions about girls who go "too far" or are "too sexy" and their condemnation of them as not respecting themselves. We also intend to look at comparable ideologies around respect and assimilation in other communities of color. We will also discuss attitudes and support or, historically, lack of support for nonheterosexual sexualities.

BLACK WOMEN'S CLUB MOVEMENT

The subject of respectability and women of color, specifically African American women, is a longstanding one, with roots dating back to the years after the Civil War. During the late 1800s and early 1900s, Black women formed social clubs, such as the National Association of Colored Women (NACW), in an attempt to eschew the image of Black womanhood as loud, emasculating, and expressing promiscuity in favor of an image of modesty and temperance, that is, respectability (Harris-Perry 2011). Still active today, the NACW states that its members are dedicated to "raising to the highest plane the home life, moral standards, and civic life of our race," and they utilize the mantra of "Lift as we 'climb'" (NACW). It is important to acknowledge the social class and access differences between women who were afforded the opportunity to join the Black women's club movement and those who were deemed to be less than respectable.

In her book, *Sister Citizen*, Melissa Harris-Perry explains that although the Black women's club movement served as a tool for political organizing around lynching and survival in post-Civil war America, these movements also focused on an image of Black women as chaste and "buried normal, innocuous expressions of sexuality behind an image of either pristine asexuality or narrowly defined respectable married identity." That is, with regard to Black women's sexuality, a binary of respectable versus not respectable was set up. It may be that given what was at stake at that time in history, a strict version of acceptable sexuality was thought to be needed. On the other hand, it may also be that Christian values intersected with ideas of protection and public impression.

Those involved in African American women's clubs offered an alternate view to Black womanhood as salacious and focused on increasing socio-economic status, respectability, and connection to the church. Club women equated respect and respectability with asexuality. This was in direct contrast to the emergence of the Blues which popularized songs that focused on Black women's sexuality and sexual desires. While many songs of Black women's desire were sexual, they contained clever lyrics (e.g., "Handy Man") and were taken up later into the popular songs and lyrics of the 1930s and 1940s, where they received more acceptance. Higginbotham (1992), the woman who coined the phrase "politics of respectability," points to the Woman's Convention (WC) of the National Baptist Convention as the first structured call for respectability The WC did many good works at the time, creating schools and orphanages, counseling prisoners, and sponsoring protests against Jim Crow laws and other racial injustices. But they reinforced an idea of personal responsibility for respectability that lives on today. In 1915 the WC's executive board wrote: "Fight segregation through the courts as an unlawful act? Yes. But [also] fight it with soap and water, hoes, spades, shovels and paint to remove any reasonable excuse for it" (Kennedy 2015).

Given this history of the respectability discourse, it is interesting to see today how African American girls negotiate the sexuality of pop stars and musicians who are sexually objectified by their public. We will discuss this to a greater extent in the next chapter, but offer here that one solution to the tension created between loving a pop star and noting that she is quite sexualized is to see her sexualization as financially beneficial to her. As money gives prestige, then sexuality and objectification are permitted to enhance that. When girls were confronted in our focus groups with this tension, either by talking about pop stars or in discussing the video, Bitch Bad, analyzed in the next chapter, they tied women's choices to financial gain. Either a poor woman needed to self-sexualize because she was being paid a lot to do so and thus had no choice but to accept such an offer, or a favorite pop star was able to lead an admirable life of fame and fortune because she permitted such displays. Both of these conceptualizations saved a woman from being considered not worthy of respect.

RESPECTABILITY POLITICS

Respectability politics is an ideology that concerns itself with the reputation, appearance, and social perception of Black people. Some describe respectability politics as an emphasis on modifying behavior and attitudes as a way to impact racial inequality and social depictions of African Americans (Higginbotham 1992). In *Black Sexual Politics*, Patricia Hill Collins argues it serves the purpose of imparting an ideal of dignity, respect, and qualities of Southern White femininity and middle-class values onto the Black body in an attempt to seek approval from one's White counterparts (Hill-Collins 2004, p. 72). But Higginbotham makes the counterargument that the politics of respectability did not produce a wholehearted imitation of the behavior and actions of the White middle-class, and instead yielded both an internal and external shifting and elevation Black social positionality (Higginbotham and Weber 1992). Both agree that power and status permit different freedom in expression.

Applied to Black female sexuality, respectability politics both heightens and limits the range of sexual expression and desire of Black girls and women. Social pressure around African American female sexuality demanded that African American women uphold a Victorian ideal of femininity; to be patient, sacrificing, but not overly vocal of their sacrifice, domestic, supportive, and dutiful (Carlson 1992; Perkin 1995).

Historically, the Moynihan Report also had something to say about Black women's respectability, something deeply problematic. The Moynihan Report, or *The Negro Family: The Case for National Action*, built upon the stereotypes of African American femininity not as overly sexual, but as emasculating, too strong, and a potentially damaging force for African American communities (Moynihan 1965). This national report advertised respectability politics as a blanket salve for the supposed ailments within African American communities. In depicting African American women as emasculating, domineering, and unfeminine, Moynihan paved the way for the concept of the respectable Black woman who is seen as subordinate and domestically supportive, as the backbone, but not the leader of Black communities (Harris-Perry 2011).

The Civil Rights movement also spoke of respectability and strategically incorporated a kind of respectability politics. According to Randall Kennedy (2015), Black people who participated in the protests of the 1960s were given "detailed instructions about what to wear (jackets for men and dresses for ladies) and how to act (be courteous and refrain from retaliating even if assaulted)." He points out that this was a measured way to show contrast between the White thugs that attacked the protesters and the dignity of the protest.

Respect in the Classroom Among Diverse Girls

The concept of respectability politics was presented within the SEC-S class dialogues. During one class session, the students and teacher engaged in a conversation about looking and dressing in a manner seen as being sexy while in high school. This topic was of great interest to one student and what ensued was a lively discussion about respectability politics, slut shaming, and power.

Teacher: Is it wrong for a girl to want to look sexy in high school? Like is it a problem?

Nija: Yeah, it is a problem actually. Like if you're going to your friend's you can wear that, but like it depends like if you need that it all depends.

Teacher: You know, don't you think that there's this really fine line that the girls have to walk that the guys don't. So like for girls you're supposed to look sexy, you're supposed to look hot for boys and things like that

Nija: You're not supposed to; you just want to.

Teacher: And then on the other hand if you look too much like that, then all the other girls and maybe the guys too are all gonna call you a slut and say like maybe you're doing too much.

Nija: I think that whenever somebody, well the reason somebody calls somebody a slut or a ho, it all starts with the girl. It doesn't have anything to do with the boy.

Teacher: What about society though?

Nija: Like in society, not just in our school but everywhere, cuz if you notice like it's the girl, like other girls are jealous and she calls the other girl a slut or a ho' cause she goes out with the boy that she really wanted to go out with, well it depends.

Teacher: There are interpersonal reasons, but society does glorify some women in ads, then puts the very same person down.

Nija: And when they do that nobody's gonna respect the person.

Alexandria: Exactly! Like what she said.

Nija: Like it can be a famous person, like even Beyoncé or something. She's out with her nipples and her boobs all out like people are gonna start not respecting her as much as she did.

Alexandria: No, like I'm sorry like you know how at the awards, Nija, the Grammy awards, she was dancing on her husband? No, like what she was wearing, like if you walk out with that like guys will be like "oh what are you wearing," but she...because she's the Queen B she can wear it.

Teacher: She has power, that's what we're talking about here. That if you have power in the world and influence, that you can probably dress the way you want,

Girls: yeah!

Teacher: But the less power you have the more you have to look respectable, in terms of the eyes of society, so that people can't call you out on those things.

In this exchange, the teacher attempts to bring a kind of discourse about the individual girl as respectable or not respectable to a discussion of society's role. The purpose of the study was to introduce talk of "we-as-a-society" into the classroom as a kind of infusion of civics education into sex education. What happened, as highlighted by Lamb and Randazzo (2016), was that a neoliberal discourse of personal choice, which echoed the ideal of "individual freedom" in democratic society, was set against the idea of being coerced or manipulated by society or the media. Adolescents preferred the discourse of individual choice. Thus, at the end of this exchange, the girls Nija and Alexandria both come to the conclusion that Beyoncé can wear whatever she wants and be respectable given her power in the world as "Queen B." Anyone else who would have "nipples and her boobs all out" would risk people not respecting her.

Some girls in the SEC-S classes and our focus groups identified as Muslim. While little research exists on Muslim girls in the United States, Naber (2006) explores the concept of sexuality and respectability from the perspective of Arab American women. We understand that all Arab American women are not Muslim and all Muslim women are not from Arabic countries; however, with so much intersectionality of race, ethnicity, religion, and class among the girls in our study, it is difficult to find research literature that matches any girl's full identity.

Similar to ideas of Black respectability politics representing the desire to achieve a similar social status of the White middle-class, Naber notes that while Arab immigrant families presented assimilation into Whiteness as an ideal, they also advocated for maintaining aspects of their Arab identity with regard to the role of family, heterosexual relationships, and assumed normative gendered behavior (Naber 2006). The concept of classy ladies is often juxtaposed with the idea of bad bitches for African American girls. Arab Americans, however, use a juxtaposition of the "good Arab girls" with "bad American girls," and the "Arab virgin" with the "American whore" (Naber 2006). Arab good girls were defined as those who upheld traditional ideals related to a cultural understanding of acceptable femininity by demonstrating a knowledge of shame, respect, piety, and familial duty. American girls, in contrast, were seen as partyers, sexualized, shameful, and disrespectful. Participants in Naber's study noted that if they were seen as possessing any of these American qualities, they were assumed to be less Arab and as having lost to American ideals (Naber 2006). A respectable young Arab woman, then, would be considered a devout heterosexual virgin.

In one of our exercises in the SECS-C, we have students choose slips of paper from a box that gives them an identity. They are then asked, if they were that particular identity (e.g., disabled; Trans; fundamental Christian), how might they view respectful conversation in the classroom. Tarria, an African American student offered: "Can I go? I got Muslim." She then offered a stereotype, "I wouldn't talk about sexiness, because they're covered head to toe."

Respectability and sexuality have also long been discussed with regard to Latina girls and women with similar dichotomies of good versus bad.

On the one hand, Latinas are seen as traditional, submissive, and virgin-like, but on the other hand, they are also seen as hypersexualized, feisty, and exotic (Juárez and Kerl 2003). These stereotypes are presented to the American public in movies, music, and literature, and may even play a part in academic, health, and policy discourses which aim to curb Latina sexualities (Zavella 2003; Garcia and Torres 2009).

This dichotomy of traditional versus sexualized is more commonly referred to as the virgin/whore dichotomy (Arrizón 2008; Everett 2000). When applied to Latinas, the "virgin/whore dichotomy" manifests in the concept of *marianismo* and/or *chonga* (Arrizón 2008; Hernandez 2009; Arrizón 2008). *Marianismo* typically refers to an ideal of respect and piety grounded in both Christian values and patriarchies. This notion most notably involves a hyperfocus on marriage before sex and sexual activities for women (Hetherington et al. 2007). *Chonga*, on the other hand, is a Spanish slang term that refers specifically to a girl who is stereotyped as promiscuous, loud, and rough (Hernandez 2009). As such, girls whose sexualities are deemed to align with *marianismo* are often seen as both more respectable and of a higher class status, while girls whose sexualities are deemed to align with the *chonga* mentality are seen as less respectable and lower class (Arrizón 2008; Hernandez 2009). There is often the belief that traditional views of Latino culture repress sexuality and the assimilation into American ideals will allow Latina adolescents to obtain a sense of sex positive liberation. However, Hernandez (2009) contends that Latina girls challenge the sexual status quo and develop a sense of agency in their sexuality by dressing in ways that correspond more toward *chonga* culture and establishing a movement away from *marianismo* (Hernandez 2009).

Very little literature exists on the sexual development of Asian American girls specifically (Chou 2012; Okazaki 2002), although the stereotype of being a "model minority" does not hold with regard to knowledge about sex and risk—they have less sex education and consequently less information (Hahm et al. 2006). Rosalind Chou (2012) writes that the sexualization of Asian American girls and women is somewhat different from that of Black women and although they are racialized their racialization is also different depending on where in Asia their family members are from, their class, and their sexuality. While women of East Asian descent have been represented as always available, exotified, and fetishized (Park 2014), women of South Asian descent are invisible or depicted as lacking sexuality at all.

There is little to tell us whether a "respectability" discourse permeates and controls Asian American teens' understanding of sexual relationships although there is some history about Chinese Americans that may apply. Around the early 1900s, considerable effort was made to "save" young girls from Chinatown and prostitution (Lui 2009), thus creating an artificial division between prostitutes and "respectable" Chinese immigrant women. And although stereotypes of Asian women are common in pornography (Dines 2010), there is no research that documents that these images reach or affect developing Asian American girls. One study, however, of Korean immigrant girls, shows them shaped by goals of intellectual achievement and promises of freedom once they reach university. Rather than promoting a feminist notion of independence, however, the purpose of intellectual achievement is quite often marriageability (Lee and Goodman 2010). We do know that many Asian American girls and women face "exotification and orientalization as sexual bodies" related to their gender (Chou 2012, p. 39) and that today and historically, marriage affirms respectability.

While much of the research on girls of color defaults to the experience of African American girls, and although these experiences and narratives are indeed informative and necessary, Black girls do not make up the entirety of girls of color. Even within the SEC-S classroom, other race, ethnicities, and identities were present such as Latina, Afro-Latina, Middle Eastern, and West Indian. The concept of respectability politics as it relates to the sexuality and sexualization of girls of color is present in ways that are both similar to and different from the Black girls' experiences.

CONTEMPORARY RESPECTABILITY POLITICS AND SEXUALITY

Tensions around respectability politics are most present today in the Black community. Randall Kennedy writes, in his article, *Lifting as We Climb* (2015), that he and his brother were raised to be "ambassadors" of Blackness (p.24). He writes, "They also told us that racism made us more vulnerable than our white counterparts to certain risks, and that we would be judged by less forgiving standards" (p. 24). Summarizing respectability politics today, he writes, "Its proponents advocate taking care in presenting oneself publicly and desire strongly to avoid saying or doing anything that will reflect badly on blacks, reinforce negative racial stereotypes, or needlessly alienate potential allies" (p. 26). Other Black intellectuals have argued that respectability politics "don't work" (Dyson 2014). As cited in Kennedy's article Brittney Cooper writes, "Black folks have already tested out . . . respectability . . . We've been trying to save our lives by dressing right, talking right and never, ever fucking up since about 1877. That shit has not worked" (p. 30). Also cited in the Kennedy article, Melissa Harris-Perry told her MSNBC audience that "no matter how appropriate their attire, respectability has never been armor against violence toward black bodies." Finally, and what seems most important, is that the discourse of respectability seems to be meeting up with a neoliberal discourse around personal responsibility in which social conditions are forgotten. Fredrick Harris notes in *Dissent* (2014), "Today's politics of respectability, however, commands blacks left behind in post–civil rights America to 'lift up thyself.'" He followed, "Respectability politics can have the effect of steering 'unrespectables' away from making demands on the state to intervene on their behalf and toward self-correction and the false belief that the market economy alone will lift them out of their plight."

With regard to sexuality, the same tensions around respectability continue to exist. For example, Ayesha Curry, celebrity cook, author, actress, popular blogger and wife of NBA star Stephen Curry, stated, "Everyone's into barely wearing clothes these days huh? Not my style. I like to keep the good stuff covered up for the one who matters," and "Just looking at the latest fashion trends. I'll take classy over trendy any day of the week. #saturdaynightinsight," These much-talked-about tweets recall the politics of respectability in the spirit of Black Women's Clubs. From her platform as not only a successful Black author and chef, but also as the wife of a NBA star, she describes women who are interested in styles considered trendy as also unknowingly promiscuous. And she makes a thinly veiled comparison to classy women who cover themselves up for modesty's sake and only show skin to "the one who matters." While not outwardly stated, there is an unspoken assumption that using one's sexuality in line with respectability politics will allow one to obtain the best marker of respectability for women: a successful heterosexual married life. This can only happen as long as women make the decision to "keep the good stuff covered up."

It's important to note that Ayesha Curry is both a woman with some power and a woman who has a lot of money, as was Beyoncé in the former example. In this way, only from a prestige position does a Black woman have the power to reinforce a very traditional view of femininity and sexuality within marriage.

CHAPTER 4

Girls of Color in Sex Education Classrooms

Abstract The central focus of this chapter explores how girls in a coed classroom deal with the vulnerability that may arise in lessons in curricula that position them as at risk for coercion and rape. Needing to assert themselves as both strong and equals to the boys in the class, they introduce ideas of retaliation and aggression. In this chapter we also discuss how girls seemingly abandon support of other girls who cross a line with regard to respect, even in situations where other girls are being exploited. Needing to maintain that a self-respecting girl should always be in control, they strongly and rather heartlessly blame other girls for putting themselves in positions where they might be raped. In the classroom they also had moments of refusing to participate in discussions of pornography, when challenged to do so. We discuss these issues in terms of the "respect" ideology, the idea that adolescents are urged to be responsible for themselves in the United States, their relationship to feminism, the historic protection of men of color by women of color when men of color have been wrongly blamed or accused of rape, and the socialization for resilience.

Keywords Sex education · Classroom · Qualitative research · Vulnerability · Class · Pornography · Girl-blaming · Othering · Religiosity · Adolescence · Peers

© The Author(s) 2016
S. Lamb et al., *Girls of Color, Sexuality, and Sex Education*,
DOI 10.1057/978-1-137-60155-1_4

In this chapter, we review sex education and what it has meant for girls of color in the United States. Then, through an analysis of our own work in the classroom with girls of color (Lamb and Randazzo 2016), we explore how girls in a coed classroom deal with the vulnerability that may arise in lessons that position them as at risk.

Recent writing on sex education focuses on the content and effectiveness of prevention programs, and this focus has been important in terms of combating Abstinence Only Until Marriage (AOUM) laws and supporting comprehensive and evidence-based practice. A focus on the preadolescents and adolescents within the classroom is rare, in spite of Michelle Fine's (1988) original work on the missing discourse of desire and notwithstanding Louisa Allen's qualitative research on New Zealand teens in sex education classes (2007, 2008). Through their work, it is clear that a focus on the students themselves and their experiences in the sex education classroom yield a different kind of information that is useful for the teacher of sex education as well as for those hoping to understand adolescents.

There has been very little research on girls of color and their experiences *in* the sex education classroom as girls of color. Because of the lack of studies on this topic, we know very little about them: their needs, reactions, and sensitivities to sex education, as well as which aspects of sex education may intersect with their experiences with racism, racialized gender, and sexual stereotypes particular to girls of color. An exception is Garcia's (2009) interviews with Mexican American and Puerto Rican girls. She discovered that teachers were overemphasizing pregnancy prevention and teaching these girls that their culture, "Latina Culture," supports early pregnancy, thus positioning their culture as problematic in comparison to White culture. She concluded that these lessons further disadvantaged girls who were already experiencing substantial social injustice. In their homes, however, Latinas talk to their mothers about sex and even show a preference for talking with their mothers (Guzmán et al., 2006) and while mothers teach about traditional gender roles, they also learn from their daughters about more liberating attitudes towards sexuality (Romo et al., 2006).

We know a bit more about the racism and injustices relating to the kinds of sex education offered to girls of color thanks to Jessica Fields' work (2005, 2008). Her interviews with the shapers of sex education curricula in North Carolina show the adults positioning girls of color as less innocent and less "vulnerable" (p. 564) than White children and orienting sex education to stop "children having children" (p. 551). Sociologist Janice Irvine (2002) noted historically that the advocacy of some of the AOUM curricula played on racial stereotypes. This racism took the form of only offering AOUM education to White communities, ignoring Black communities, or by combatting curricula that specifically addressed diversity education such as the "Children of the Rainbow" curriculum (Irvine 2002, p. 155).

Froyum (2010) argued that in sex education curricula, particularly the AOUM curricula of the past three decades, Black girls were positioned by teachers as especially vulnerable not only to pregnancy but to sex and desire. In her research, she documented teachers framing sexual restraint as a matter of morality and in so doing reinforcing traditional gender stereotypes and gender inequalities. African American female teachers of African American students professed that sexuality made girls vulnerable to rape, STIs, and pregnancy, transforming "girls' physical capability and desire for sexual expression and childbearing into burdens" (Froyum, 2010, p. 63). The teachers also construed motherhood as a life full of abandonment, burden, and loneliness.

In Froyum's study, the sex education teachers followed the teachings on respect that came out of the tradition described in Chap. 3. They taught girls of color that *looking presentable* and *putting yourself together in a respectful manner* were the answers to the inherently risky and immoral prospect of sexuality. These Black teachers exaggerated a vulnerability discourse to encourage girls to control their own bodies rather than to encourage girls into activism that would bring about greater access to birth control, respect for single mothers, and better rape prevention in their communities.

We have written elsewhere about the limitations of the evidence-based approach to sexuality education (Lamb 2013a), arguing that this approach handles "just the facts" (meaning contraception and STI prevention), whereas important issues regarding how to treat other people and how to understand sex in society are left out because these topics haven't been shown to assist in prevention. In response to this omission, we have also developed and delivered a curriculum that addresses this lack through practical philosophy lessons and democratic discussion of issues like consent, rape, pornography, and media objectification (Lamb 2013b). The "Sexual Ethics for a Caring Society Curriculum" (SECS-C) is a feminist curriculum designed for a coed classroom of high school students. It has been carried out in seven different coed classrooms in the United States with primarily 9th graders.

Through our experience teaching the SECS-C (2013b) curriculum to students of color, we began to pick up on resistances from the girls in particular. We came to understand this not only as resistance but as an expression of vulnerability that we began to believe may have something to do with the intersection of race and gender (Crenshaw et al. 2015).

We understand vulnerability to be multiply determined and, from a psychodynamic perspective, to be experienced consciously as well as unconsciously (Mitchell and Black 1995). We also understand the students as adolescents, constructing who they are and what they feel through multiple identity positions that they develop within the specific context of their school, country, ethnicity, race, ability status, and gender. The unconscious vulnerabilities, understood through psychoanalytic and cultural theory, derive from that which, in adolescence, might be unacceptable to the self (Freud 1936/1993; Mitchell and Black 1995). For example, for some adolescent girls, sexual desire may be unacceptable and attempts might be made to keep such desire out of conscious awareness. Another example of material that might be kept out of conscious awareness is girls' vulnerability to rape. This is supported by a culture in which rape statistics are suppressed and there is widespread acceptance of rape myths (Franiuk et al. 2008; Payne et al. 1999). Our students also have unconscious vulnerabilities (along with the conscious vulnerabilities) relating to minority status and past as well as continued racism experienced in the present.

The girls became a focus in our research group because of troubling comments they made. These were common among the different classes and conversations that we had about sex and sexuality, independent of which teacher they had, and we sought to understand these comments from a position of intersectionality. That is, we believed that the intersection of gender, race, and ethnicity might be playing a part in production of this discourse. We found the students curious, interested, engaged, savvy, and sometimes frustrating. But we also, as Counseling Psychology students and a professor, were cognizant of other dynamics in the students. We explore their vulnerability with regard to several feminist topics that are central to the curriculum. These topics regarding consent, media objectification, pornography, and rape are topics of great concern to feminists and the prevention of sexual violence. Yet these topics were the topics about which the girls of color had the strongest and surprisingly misogynist views.

We piloted the SECS-C in a Boston area Charter school over a 2-year period with seven racially diverse groups of adolescents in 9th grade classes called "Advisories." The participating school asked us to provide eight lessons from the SECS-C, delivering one per week for 1 hr, to seven groups of 9th graders (comprising two entire 9th grade cohorts over 2 years' time). There were 15–20 students in each of the 7 classes with slightly more girls than boys in each. Students were aged 13–16.

Three-quarters of the students in our classes had at least one parent who was an immigrant to the United States. The students identified were non-White Latino, African American, Indian, and at the same time children of immigrant parents or immigrants themselves from Africa, the Caribbean, Central America, and South America. The students also reportedly came from Catholic, Protestant, and Muslim families, according to the school counselor. In terms of race, 47% identified themselves as Black or African American, 22% as Latino or Hispanic and Non-White, 8% as Latino or Hispanic and White, 4% as White, 1% as Asian, 1% as Native American, and 15% as "Other." Fifty-six percent of the sample qualified for a free lunch.

The students and their parents had the opportunity to "opt out" of the course but few did.

The teachers of the seven classes were: a Jewish, White female professor in her late 50s (one section); a White woman in her early 30s (three sections); an African American woman in her late 20s (one section); a White woman in her late 20s (one section); and another White woman in her late 20s (one section). They were of varying sexual orientations and came from both middle and working class backgrounds.

As we noted in the introduction, theorists have expressed concerns that, when qualitative researchers represent the marginalized others' voices and experiences without reflexivity, they may produce a "colonizing discourse of the other," "occluding themselves and their own investments" (Henwood 2008, p. 49). To address this concern, reflexive researchers are called upon to reveal their identities and make themselves vulnerable, which we deem most appropriate in a paper exploring vulnerability. We were older (than the students), feminist-identified, female teachers, all but one of whom are White. Our own histories of oppression and privileges (in relation to the students and as perceived by students) affected the dynamics of the SECS-C classrooms. The commonalities between teachers and students included experiences with sexual harassment, abuse, and assault. And we had connections within our own family backgrounds with regard to immigration, poverty, and other intersecting identities.

We met in a café before teaching the lessons. There we teachers reflected on our own histories, including privilege, histories of oppression, race, and class. We also explored to what extent these interacted with students' histories and expectations as well as our own. Tangela Roberts, second author, was whom the White teachers turned to in order to see if discussions in her class differed from discussions in their own class. When the discussion differed, we would consider together whether race played a part. As noted earlier, the democratic classroom was emphasized and an introductory lesson had students come up with a plan for how discussions would be run and how disruptions would be handled. Students could opt out of the course or any particular class and were treated as willing participants encouraged to speak their minds.

The charter school that gave us the opportunity to teach the curriculum was situated in a neighborhood that had many immigrant families; because of its reputation for placing students in colleges and firm discipline, it also drew students from around this Boston suburb. There was a system of demerits in the classroom that served to control student behavior and focus them on the work at hand. These demerits were handed out freely and at one parent meeting the second author attended, parents had complaints about how often the school was calling home. The school also encouraged students to snap when someone in the class said something smart or something with which they agreed. The exact racial demographics of the teachers at the school was undocumented by the research team, but we observed that the majority of the students were of color and the majority of their teachers, approximately 3/4, appeared to be White.

The three forms of resistance that we discuss here came from three kinds of experiences noticed by all teachers. The first was a felt sense of discomfort in the classroom by the teachers with regard to a refusal to discuss certain subjects. The second was a tendency to equalize vulnerabilities as if boys' and girls' vulnerabilities in sexual situations were equivalent. The third form of resistance was a tendency in discussion to blame girls if they had been exploited or even raped.

REFUSING TO ENTER THE CONVERSATION

We know that the issue of voice is complicated by race, ethnicity, and class, and that self-silencing may be related to these intersecting identities (Iglesias and Cormier 2002). Thus, we explored silencing of the girls that occurred from this perspective. The curriculum begins with fun topics such as liking, loving, and lusting after others and ties these topics to religious history, psychology, and sociology. When we moved to topics such as consent, coercion, objectification, and pornography, however, we were surprised by the frequency and intensity of female students' resistance to what we saw as feminist positions. The pornography lesson comes after the lesson on objectification, and while it does not take a pro- or antiporn stand per se, it raises questions about the ethics around pornography. In several classes, female students seemed to talk among themselves in the classroom but refused to participate publicly. In one class, they appeared to be angry with the teacher. After class, this teacher asked the female students why they had acted angry in class and why they wouldn't speak up. One replied that the girls were disgusted by the whole subject. They were angry that the teacher would even bring it up in school. This was also seen in one of the early comments in the classroom when one girl said porn was "nasty." There may have been an assumption that in a conversation about porn, boys were privileged. In fact, such conversations in the classrooms did give the boys the opportunity to laugh about porn and throw out examples that were embarrassing to the girls in the class. After the teacher asked if pornography gave viewers the wrong ideas about what is pleasurable in sex, Tomás said, "Most women don't want to get drenched on their face." Although true, this may have been exactly the cavalier and even disrespectful talk that the girls in the class were afraid would occur.

Although this incident occurred in the first author's classroom, another teacher recalled her own discomfort with sex education during her adolescence, flashing back to a memory of crying over the prospect of discussing something so intimate in a classroom full of disrespectful male peers. One teacher noted that in her classroom, the boys who were seated in the back of her class were not participating, but laughing amongst themselves as she presented objectified images of women for discussion in that lesson.

We came to understand this not simply as girls' vulnerability in the face of boys' power and privilege around pornography, but as their own bid for power in the classroom through clamming up. The boys could show off for other boys regarding what they knew already, laugh at the images rather than express some concern or anger at demeaning aspects, and rest easily in the privileged position that these images were created for them to enjoy or reject. The girls exerted the power to not participate. Some researchers (Taylor et al. 1995) found that girls of color disconnected from their teachers by 10th grade. We believe the girls sensed their vulnerability in the face of this privilege of the boys and perhaps of their White teachers. Rather than opt for what the teachers would describe as a more powerful position of feminist critique of these images, they rallied around a more conservative or even religious position of the images being "nasty" and suggested it was disrespectful to talk about them in the classroom.

EQUALIZING TENDENCIES

Philosopher Lawrence Blum (2012), writing about racism, refers to what he calls arguments based on "false symmetries." Blum explains that false symmetries occur when students make arguments that put different moral wrongs on an equal footing when if one were to consider background conditions, the wrongs are not equal. Blum notes that students sometimes describe discrimination against Whites as on the same moral footing as discrimination against Blacks because both involve "discrimination 'on the basis of race'" (p. 649). But, he argues, the identities belonging to the person who is discriminated against matter with regard to determining the extent of the harm and the wrong. We write elsewhere (Lamb and Randazzo 2016) as does Bay-Cheng and Eliseo-Arras (2008) about how this equalizing tendency fits with a neoliberal project in sex education, one that elevates individual choice and freedom.

In the SECS-C classrooms, both female and male students would counter an example of male privilege with a hypothetical situation—or "I heard of" situation—of females wielding power over males. They produced false symmetries to equalize gender-based vulnerability. One example came from a conversation about male violence against women:

Sarena: Isn't it a double standard in marriage that guys are the ones who do domestic violence and women don't?
Teacher: What do you all think, is that true?
Sarena: Yeah, and it's like women might not hit their men, but they do other things, it's like they'll hurt their men in other ways. (Sounds of approval in the classroom.)

Another example came from a conversation about nonconsensual sex:

Edgar: But sometimes you can be in at the moment but then like the next day you don't remember anything because you blacked out.

Jasmine: But I feel like girls are not always the victims. Like yeah guys have muscles and they're bigger than us, but it's like girls can do bad stuff to guys, too. Like a girl can lie about her age to get the guy incarcerated. (Sounds of approval in the classroom.)

A third came in conversations about objectification:

Frank: It's also for guys, too. Like if you see Abercrombie and Hollister, you see guys with six packs, and it's like I can't look like that.

Genevieve: Yeah I went on Black Friday and there was a guy there sitting with no shirt on. Like an *actual guy.*

The girls and boys clearly reflect patriarchal culture which orients individuals toward making invisible the harm to women through rape, sexualization, and objectification. They also, more generously, may have had simple notions of democratic ideals and tried to even the score, creating a more comfortable classroom where everyone is to blame and no one has to sit uncomfortably in their identity. The girls quite probably want to see themselves as fair, and not prejudiced.

We think that some of these objections might also be coming from a place of self-protection with regard to the vulnerability of girls' bodies to being raped, objectified, and abused. In several classes, for example, girls would bring up having heard about some sort of contraption that essentially was an "anti-rape female condom." The description was of a condom that fit inside a girl's vagina and that had little daggers sticking out of it so that if a man were to attempt to rape her, his "pickle," as one girl called it, would be cut up. The mention of this, in discussions of coercion and rape, served to position the girls as strong and as fighters, invulnerable if not savvy and prepared.

Darlene: I have a story. There was a girl who was going to have sex with a guy and he told her she was sexy beforehand, and she got mad, and she put a cone in herself that was the size of his pickle, but it had spikes on it, and so when they had sex, his pickle got slashed. But like, he had gotten her drunk, and he thought she was a prostitute.

The violent nature of this imagery that came in response to a comment about girls' vulnerability reflects the intensity of female students' discomfort in the classroom.

At times, statements seemed to function as warning to male peers not to assume weakness on the part of females.

> *Anna:* I'm speaking for myself. I think some guys, not all guys, they think that girls are, like, soft, and they don't have walls built up around them. That they just give in easily. So I think that if a guy is extremely nice and buys a lot of things for the prom, if he thinks she's going to give him sex, I would be pissed off. It's because he thinks that girls are soft.

Here, the students' intent seems clearly directed at her peers, illuminating one underlying motivation for female students' resistance to discussing gender inequity.

In these conversations, we teachers felt uncomfortable reinforcing the fact that girls and women do get raped, in spite of such inventions, that these condoms are not common, (if they exist at all), and that any feeling of empowerment from such a contraption might be false. We discussed whether in the neighborhoods where these girls came from, toughness and displays of toughness was an empowered position and did serve as a kind of protection. It also took the focus off boys and men as rapists. The problem became not how to prevent boys and men from exploiting girls and women, but how to make girls strong enough to protect themselves. This kind of conversation was held with much delight among the girls, thus also supporting that this talk helped them not to be positioned as vulnerable in front of their male peers.

GIRL BLAMING

Much to the dismay of the feminist-identified SECS-C teachers, girls' resistance often took the form of girl blaming when they encountered examples of female sexual exploitation. In a class discussion of the 2012 rape case in Steubenville, Ohio, for example, female students insisted on blaming the victim in their assessments of moral responsibility.

> *Glenda:* Everybody who was at the party, it's everyone's fault. Like first of all, why would you do something like that? And taking pictures

and videos, like obviously people are going to see it. If you didn't
want to get caught why would you do that? Secondly, it's wrong,
it's everyone else's fault for not trying to stop it. Like you see this
girl being paraded around naked. It's her friend's fault for not
bringing her home if she was drunk and passed out. And it's her
fault for drinking in the first place. (sounds indicating agreement
from peers)

Audra: Break it down, girl!

Glenda: And in the beginning, I saw that people were saying that it was
her fault, or whatever. And it wasn't her fault that she got raped,
but it was her fault for getting drunk.

While encouraging students to consider the ethical failure of the perpe-
trator and the society that would condone this ethical failure, we as
teachers often struggled with statements that placed blame on the victim.
As we talked to each other and processed the teaching experiences, we
began to understand that female students were working to position the
sexual assault victim as "other," distancing themselves from the vulnerability to such violence.

Blaming of girls also occurred in terms of dressing in such a way as to
provoke boys' naturalized sexual desire. In a contradictory way, they first
argued that girls should have the option to wear whatever they want to
wear and not be policed by anyone, particularly the school. On the other
hand, they used a respectability discourse to argue that girls need to be
limited by notions of what is respectable dress because if they do not
conform to what is generally considered to be respectable dress, they
may provoke boys.

Juan: What I'm trying to say is guys can't hold back what they do
so they're obviously going to say something. When you're
saying that guys shouldn't say anything, if you saw this
from a guy's perspective you would know how...

Maeve: They should be able to dress how they want, but they should
do so with moderation. They should be able to express themselves, but they are women, so there's a limit to how much
they can.

Samantha: All right so, I get what Juan's trying to say like if a girl is wearing
whatever she wants to wear and it's too much that whoever is
thinking about not getting her consent... I understand that.
But a person needs to know what they can and can't do, and

what they should or should not do. Like I'm a female and you so if you're exposing yourself, that's on you, but you have to know what can come with it. You have to know what the consequences of your actions are.

Juan: They're not asking for anything ... they did want a little bit of attention ... but they like the clothes that they were wearing, too. I don't think you're really asking for it unless you're wearing ... I'm trying to talk about moderation and being, like elegant. Like there's a limit on how much skin you should show.

Boys and men are constructed as sexual initiators who sometimes "can't hold back." Any challenge to boys' sexual entitlement is usurped within the discourse that places full responsibility on girls and women to dress with moderation. Additionally, caught between the competing demands to resist male desire (and hence remain respectable) and create a sense of sexual allure to keep up with popular culture and expectations of their peers, girls of color end up in a no-win situation.

Students often "othered" girls they were condemning. This "othering," as a discursive strategy, is a way to position themselves through discourse in relation to the other girls. It was used by female students not only to distance themselves from sexual desire, but also to distance themselves from vulnerability to the harms of media influence. One exception to this trend, especially notable because of the scarcity of such statements, was an instance when a female student entered the risky discursive territory of reflecting on her own vulnerability. In a discussion about rape myths, including the notion that "if a woman doesn't fight back, it isn't really rape," the student bravely commented:

Jasmine: Like you know how you get really scared and freeze, and what if she doesn't know what to do and she's really scared and her mind is like she really wants to fight and run away but she just stands there and can't move. There was a point where I was hit by a car and I just stood there, instead of walking up the street I just stood there cause I was scared, it was like I froze. It wasn't voluntary. So she's scared and there's this really weird guy trying to rape her and she says no but she's too scared to move her butt and she's just, what's that word? Do you understand what I'm trying to say?

As she concluded her story by asking for understanding, she strove to bring home her point that fear can cause paralysis. Illustrated with a self-disclosure about her own traumatic experience, this comment stands out in the context of defensive positioning that characterized all seven rounds the SECS-C classrooms.

REASONS FOR RESISTANCE

The girls were resisting some of the feminist lessons for different reasons. Refusing to talk about pornography positioned them as more mature and respectable than the boys. Discussion of female condoms that injured men's penises in attempted rape appeared to be a show of strength and equality with boys' power to harm. It was also a show of invulnerability. And girl-blaming in situations when a girl gets raped appeared to be a way to preserve choice, agency, and responsibility, asserting that respectable girls don't get raped.

The feminist teachers may have found themselves struggling against competing discourses that addressed vulnerability. Introducing a discourse around critical consciousness, solidarity, the blaming of social forces, and activism, that is, a feminist discourse that pointed students outwards toward other people and society, hit up against a discourse of self-protection through pride and respect, a religious discourse of respectability, and an individualizing discourse.

Isom's (2012) qualitative work with youth of color showed femaleness constructed as "strong, multitudinous and varied, yet sexualized by a male gaze and silent in the face of it" (p. 127). Indeed, 5th grade female students of color professed their strength and control, but often remained silent about the realities of sexism. When the girls in Isom's study first encountered being sexualized by the boys through their language or behavior they became silent; but in a second study they responded with "verbal proofs of their purity, their virginity" (p. 133). Isom writes that for girls connected to a church, sexual purity seemed to operate as a source of social power, "enabling them to talk back to boys and put down other girls" (p. 133).

The vociferousness with which girls attacked other girls who went too far or who were sexual in possibly positive ways (e.g., not the girl who was drunk and exploited), may have been a way to distance themselves from sexual desire. Although researchers note that students *want* sex education classes to teach them about pleasure, it is a topic that may make them feel vulnerable. In an analysis of the discourse around sexuality within a group of young Black women in the United Kingdom, Weekes (2002) showed the ways in which women excluded themselves entirely from sexual desire, sometimes by denigrating peers who express sexuality. In the SECS-C classrooms, too, sexual desire was frequently "othered," sometimes in ways that were raced. A comment from a male student that "White girls are easy" in one class induced a flurry of animated responses, with some peers calling out racism and others voicing their support. Overall, the underlying sentiment that Black girls are not easy was one that seemed to sit comfortably within the discourse of respectability, but which again cost young women of color any opportunity to talk about experiencing or expressing desire.

Research on religious African Americans has shown that religiosity can be perceived as adaptive in environments with acute of chronic stress (Utsey et al. 2008). Religion may have played a role in the respectability discourse, but not always in sole reference to Christianity. Two Muslim students, in separate classes, were among the strongest voices. In the first author's classroom, A'Ida took on a perspective that blamed the media for objectifying and sexualizing material, acknowledging (which was rare in these classes) that media might be damaging in terms of its effects on sexual development. Coming from a family that did not permit her to watch the same TV as her peers and who had strict prohibitions about other activities such as wearing makeup and sexy clothing (so she said in class), her perspective from a systematic religious and family view appeared to enable her to take an outsider position that supported critique.

Perhaps simply being an adolescent set the girls in opposition to the feminist women teachers. Adolescence is known to be a time of increased striving for autonomy (Erikson 1966; Garrod et al. 2005), and gender, racial, ethnic, and sexual identities add complexity to these strivings (Garrod et al. 2005). According to Lesko (2012), adolescence itself is "raced," in that identity formation as a person of color characterizes the teen years in important ways. The yearning for peer acceptance is particularly strong in adolescence, and Duncan (2005) talks about how Black peer groups can be comforting to their members because they provide answers to perplexing questions related to race and identity, questions that neither White peers nor adult family members can adequately address. Drawing on W. E. B. Du Bois' early writing on "double consciousness" (1903), Isom (2012) writes that "moving between projected images and constructed versions of identity, the Black youth finds her/himself on an ever-shifting playing ground for authentic identity development" (p. 128).

Another consideration as we examine the dialogue in the SECS-C classrooms is the interplay of student identities with intersecting identities of the teachers. The teachers held positions of authority. Furthermore, the teachers, like the teachers in the charter school, were predominantly White (although the African American teacher experienced the same resistance). Youth of color may have understood that teachers as authority figures were invested in controlling their sexuality rather than collaborating with them. Indeed, a class lesson on pleasure in which the teachers emphasized sexual pleasure as an important goal and essential right, came at the end of eight classes. It is also possible that the teachers' feminism, entering into the classroom through discussion as it naturally would, was perceived at times by students as threats to their own worldviews.

While these resistances may have been a defense against unconscious vulnerabilities, they might also represent a public voice in relation to the classroom dynamics. It may very well be that the students were aware of their vulnerabilities and chose to represent their views in the ways they did to consciously protect themselves in an unsafe atmosphere. In all classes, there was a dynamic in which some very vocal students held sway of public opinion. Thus, the vulnerability to speak out from a feminist perspective and risk being seen as different might have been particularly strong in the 9th grade. In one class, there was one African American girl who would strongly present girl-blaming statements. It seemed as if her power and prestige silenced other girls such that ironically, only the boys were allowed to express feminist opinions. In the second author's classroom, there was a boy who played class clown and who stated extremely non-feminist opinions often interrupting others to share. When students were encouraged to argue against these, they seemed uncertain about how to do so.

While the discourse of respectability and the defensive ways that girls positioned themselves as empowered in the classroom was protective, we understood these as students' growth into new awareness. The politics of respectability, it has been argued, is rooted in racism and can function in detrimental ways for all people of color (Duncan 2005). For us its ramifications on girls of color in relation to sexuality were most perceptibly oppressive. Like the virgin/whore dichotomy deployed to demonize White female sexual expression, the respectable Black woman/whore dichotomy serves to keep girls and women of color from the potential of experience of sexuality and sexual expression. It also was .1 in a hostile tone toward other girls, which is interesting given .quity of slut-shaming discourses (Brown 2003; Ringrose and .1 2012). As Harris (2003) writes of the "gatekeeping" function of resp. .ctability discourses, can't "respectability" be achieved without comparisons to other girls?

Batchelor (2006) argues, the voice of control in the classroom can function to erase possibilities for an ontological voice of becoming, of openness to growth and new ideas. According to Batchelor, the positive potential of vulnerability as a factor in students' learning is understated. Rather than defining vulnerability negatively as weakness, low status, or lack of control, vulnerability can refer to exposure, an undefendedness that can be a positive form of openness. Creating safe spaces for vulnerable voices in a sex education classroom is difficult, and perhaps made more so by the specific intersectionalities of our pilot project of teaching the SECS-C. However, without attempts to do so, young people will not be challenged to open up to new ways of thinking. Sex education dedicated to attentiveness to complex identities and classroom dynamics is needed, in hopes that teachers can help students find the courage to celebrate the potential of new ways of thinking, acknowledging the vulnerabilities that accompany marginalization, as well as the responsibilities that accompany power.

CHAPTER 5

Girls of Color and the Media

Abstract We use this chapter to discuss the literature on media influences and the sexualization of girlhood. With a focus on the literature addressing girls of color we also review some of the debate about the genre of hip-hop. We provide a literature review on the effects of media and critique this literature using Rosalind Gill's analysis. Within this chapter we also discuss how we used a Lupe Fiasco video to explore the effects of media on girls and boys of color and how our students responded to it.

Keywords Media influence · Social media · Confidence · Performance · Hypersexualization · Hip hop · Minstrel shows · Media literacy · Heteronormativity · Commodification · Objectification

In our last chapter and in previous work (Lamb et al. 2016), we wrote about a Muslim girl in one of our focus groups who was quite savvy about objectification of girls and women by the media. She had critical consciousness about the media as representing mainstream stereotypes of gender and race, and she proclaimed loudly that she was no dupe. She was, in fact, a leader in the conversation about media objectification and did not blame individual girls for how they acted or dressed as did other girls in the group. But this girl also used as an example of women who "own" their sexuality that we found surprising: the Victoria's Secret fashion models whom she had recently seen walk the runway in lingerie on

© The Author(s) 2016
S. Lamb et al., *Girls of Color, Sexuality, and Sex Education*,
DOI 10.1057/978-1-137-60155-1_5

the yearly TV special in which they are featured. She noted that she saw these women as positive role models, "not because they're marketing lingerie, but just the way they strut their stuff... they're really comfortable in their own skin and I really like that."

Gill (2007) suggests that the media idealizes sexual empowerment in an uncomplicated way, and our research participant reduced this idea of empowerment to "confidence." But this is not only an example of the "schizoid" subjectivity of girls today in relation to sexualization and the media (Renold and Ringrose 2011). What's complicated here is that inclusion of a woman of color on the runway is also seen as a sign of progress: that a woman of color can walk the Victoria's Secret runway and "own it," like any White woman, is considered a coup for racial justice. At the same time, a performance of "confidence" and "owning it" is a statement, to girls everywhere, that they need not be ashamed of being a sexual person. This may be particularly important to girls of color whose family cultures would have them denying sexuality until marriage. Finally, as adolescents, often insecure about how they look or how others perceive them, see it, to simply have the courage to put oneself out there on the runway, looks empowering. Thus, girls' responses to the media is complicated, and, we must recall Gill's warning that all media is not mainstream and that girls make media and interact with media, never drinking it straight from the bottle, so to speak.

RESEARCH ON MEDIA INFLUENCES

It is clear to many today that media convey information about social expectations about both gender and sexuality and that this information has the capacity to bestow social worth on those who meet such expectations (Gunter 2012; Halliwell and Diedrichs 2012). The appearance ideal (defined in Chap. 2), narrowly defined as thin, White, and Western, is also often hypersexualized (APA Task Force on the Sexualization of Girls, 2007; Murnen and Smolak 2012; Szymanski et al. 2011) and reduces the value of women to their sexual appeal (Fredrickson and Roberts 1997).

One way some media establishes worth is simply through visibility. Who is on TV? Who is permitted a sex scene in the movie? Who dances in the music video? Mainstream media still, however, has very few depictions of girls of color as sexual beings although social media and music videos abound with these. The lack of girls of color as developing sexual beings in mainstream media helps us to understand how the girl of color, a Muslim girl, in our first example can both criticize the objectification of women by the media while at the same time applauding the sponsor for making visible that women of color can be sexy.

Many researchers who study girls, their opinions, and their discourse have noted that girls do not consider themselves dupes of the media (Jackson and Vares 2015; Lamb et al 2016; Squires et al. 2006) and have learned to critique it. As Durham (2004) notes in her research on South Asian Immigrant girls, their critique of media positions them as more knowledgeable than their parents whom they perceive as buying wholesale versions of girls gone wild, and which is at the root of their parents' angst concerning their freedoms. Durham (2004) notes that "the girls believed their own oppositional decoding of the television text was diametrically opposed to their parents' dominant reading" (p. 152). Coy (2009), in her focus group, also found "resisters" in online media:

> The Resisters subverted media stereotypes about Black girls and created their own safe spaces within a homophobic online peer culture saturated with contradictory messages. In this regard, Resisters follow in the tradition of Black female performers, songwriters, and producers who challenge controlling images of Black womanhood within blues, rap, and R&B music through resistant narratives and counter discourses within the male-dominated music industry.

French (2013) noted a discourse of "personal responsibility" and argued that perhaps girls would only focus on areas that were in their control whereas changing society or even how Black males treated them was not.

Much of the analysis about the effects of media on Black girls' sexuality have focused on hip-hop music (Love 2012; Stephens and Phillips 2003, 2005; Stokes 2007; West 2009). Earlier feminist work in this area (Morgan 1995, 2000) discussed the way in which hip-hop is sold as a "singularly cathartic space where black men, in particular, can honestly express and, therefore, work through their pain" but which offered "limited modes of identification to women" (as cited in Lindsey 2013, p. 24). Hip hop feminism, on the other hand, and in the words of Joan Morgan, "attempts to navigate the complicated but interwoven terrains of racism, classism, patriarchy, sexism, ableism misogyny, homophobia, and a politics of pleasure and sexual erotics" (as cited in Lindsey 2013, p. 24). But hip hop feminism is a small branch of a large tree.

Stephens and Phillips (2003, 2005), using sexual script theory, presented six highly stereotyped African American women scripts as seen in mainstream hip-hop media: the "Gold Digger," "the Diva," "Freak," and also "Dyke," "Gangster Bitch," "Sister Savior," "Earth Mother," and "Baby Mama." To the sexualized roles, Ross and Coleman (2011) added the "Video Girl," who is distinguished from the "Gold Digger" in that the gold digger is "using her sexuality in order to obtain and maintain material provisions" and the video girl is using "her sexuality for professional gain" (p. 165). Thus, a differentiation was made by girls and young women regarding the bad girl/gold digger and good girl/ professional.

The conflicts between applauding a woman who gets ahead by making money off of her sexuality and deriding a woman who sells her body are complicated and embedded in discussions of hip-hop in general. Miller-Young (2008) writes of the "profound anxiety within 'the Black community' over the moral and political value of contemporary mainstream hip-hop cultural production" (p. 265). She writes of the links between the porn industry and the hip-hop industry, marketing "subversive sexualities to consumers" for enormous profit. She sees racialized desire as both transgressive and policed, asking if we can move beyond always seeing hip-hop as dangerous and damaging while at the same time acknowledging that it is responsible for the "iconographic and material sexual abuse of black women" as described by Parreñas Shimizu (2005, p. 266). She goes on to talk about how the black "ho" is not as invisible as Black women of diverse sexualities (in hip-hop) and constructed as not entirely powerless victims and not entirely blameless agents. But as Sharpley-Whiting (2007) writes, regarding choice and autonomy, for "video ho's" the choice is not the woman's independent choice and "Black women's sexuality in the marketplace of hip hop ... is then devalued and heavily discounted" (p. 66).

This idea of choice and autonomy, echoing the neoliberalism of our students' comments in the last chapter and in what follows, stands out in discussions of Rihanna's experience of domestic violence at the hands of partner Chris Brown. An Afro-Carribbean woman, Rihanna (Robyn) needed to maintain an image of her music and public persona as sex-positive and offering "differing desires and relationship structures, and individual choices based on consent" (Queen and Comella 2008, p. 275). But, as Esther Jones (2013) writes, this cornered Rihanna into a position in which she needed to invest considerable creative energy into "challenging the label of victim assigned to her after the event by reinforcing another stereotype: that of the hypersexual bad black woman" (p. 78). She attempted to undermine the disempowering images of her "by using a sexual script already overdetermined by stereotypes of black women's illicit sexuality and dominant cultural scripts about the misogynistic and violent underpinnings of hip-hop/rap culture" (p. 81). Squires et al. (2006) also notes, Black girls are encouraged to be more self-reliant and to distance themselves from the label of victim, thus, her response to abuse is complicated.

EFFECTS ON GIRLS AND SOCIETY

As noted in Chap. 1, limitations in the expression and experience of sexuality for girls and women of color are related to historical views of Black female sexuality, including the history of the Hottentot Venus and the stereotype of the Jezebel (Henderson 2014; Ross and Coleman 2011, Stephens and Phillips 2003). For Latina women, the stereotypes are related to being passionate, hot-blooded, and flirtatious (Jiminez and Abreu 2003).

Music videos in particular often reinforce gender norms and sexuality (Jhally Killoy, Bartone, and Media Education Foundation 2007), and, some argue, they influence youth's expectations around gender and sex (Ward et al. 2005). Influence of such music videos on youth attitudes about sex and violence have been demonstrated, with both female and male participants who viewed music videos of highly objectified female artists reporting more adversarial sexual beliefs and more acceptance of interpersonal violence (Aubrey et al. 2011). Among girls, self-objectification (Fredrickson and Roberts 1997) may mediate the relationship between music television viewing and diminished body esteem, dieting, depressive symptoms, anxiety, and lower confidence in math ability (Grabe and Hyde 2009). Among boys, viewing highly sexual music videos correlates with greater objectification of women, sexual permissiveness, stereotypical gender attitudes, and acceptance of rape (Arganbright and Lee 2007). In addition, hip-hop fandom plays a significant role in youth's objectification of women and sexual permissiveness (Arganbright and Lee 2007). A longitudinal study examining exposure to music lyrics showed that greater exposure led to earlier engagement in heterosexual intercourse (Martino et al. 2006). And we know that when Black girls internalize the message that Black women are oversexed and need to be controlled, this is associated with greater propensity toward sexual risk-taking behaviors (Townsend et al. 2010). Mainstream literature that looks narrowly at physical and psychological symptoms has shown that buying into media ideals is associated with increased risk for depression, anxiety, body dissatisfaction, disordered eating, and low self-esteem, (APA 2007; Stice 2002; Stice et al. 2001). The objectification of girls and women is also associated with discriminatory practices and increased sexist attitudes toward women (Mundorf et al. 2007) as well as increased violence against women (Hald et al. 2010). And those who objectify girls and women also see them as less competent (Murnen and Smolak 2012).

Critics of this mainstream literature (which includes the APA report on the Sexualization of Girls) and what has been called a "moral panic" about childhood innocence with regard to the sexual development for girls (Egan and Hawkes 2008; Lerum and Dworkin 2009) point to the way girls are positioned in this literature as passively receiving messages which they internalize and then enact. Instead, girls must be seen not only as passive, but also as agents who negotiate complicated messages.

As noted earlier, it's important to understand that this research on media influences occurs in the context of a larger conversation about girls' empowerment, one in which some, including girls themselves, "champion aspects of 'sexualized' culture such as pornography, burlesque or the popularity of pole dancing" (Gill 2012, p. 736) as empowering. Gill notes that so often when we critique media and its sexualizing effect on girls, we forget that girls are increasingly involved in media as producers of it and that media involves more than tv and movies. It includes playing online games, tweeting, and using Facebook and Youtube. She reminds us that the idea of "straightforward imitation" has long been abandoned in media studies (p. 739).

Others use what students love, even problematic media, to capture their interest and inspire them. Bettina Love (2012, 2013, 2014) advocates for the use of hip hop with girls in classrooms who identify with hip hop culture. She argues that knowledge becomes an embodied practice with the use of hip hop, a participation in their heritage. If this is a cultural legacy, they then can connect with pride to their past which contributes to success in the future. Rather than calling this empowerment, she notes Angela Duckworth's (2016) work on "grit," defined as persistence, and connects this to social and emotional intelligence of girls in the classroom, also describing this as at the root of hip hop.

Lindsey (2013) takes a look at both damaging and empowering media made for and about African American girls. She uses the example of a video that went viral of an under-aged girl performing oral sex, a video that is legally child pornography. After this video went viral the online discussions condemned the girl as a slut or a ho and blamed the sexualization of culture (rather than seeing her as a victim of it). Lindsey notes that "Despite her status as an adolescent, the racialized, gender stereotype of the hypersexual black woman became central to her framing within digital and social media" (p. 25).

In contrast she discusses two positive Black female videos, the Sesame Street video "I love my hair" and Willow Smith's debut single "Whip my Hair." In the latter Smith is surrounded by multiracial girls whipping their hair in an effort to embrace "their individuality and self-expressivity." A subversive aspect of the video is that a trans woman, Mizrahi, plays the role of the teacher. Lindsey notes that "Black hair, as both an industry and as a discourse, has a long and contentious history within the African diaspora, and specifically within black communities that encounter White/Eurocentric beauty standards as aesthetic ideals" (p. 27). But why is pride associated with pride in looks and not with sexuality? Why is it associated with hair more so than the Black body?

The lack of visibility of Asian American girls results in Americanization and exoticization as overlapping processes so that they not only learn to be sexual, but they learn to play on stereotypes of Asian girl sexuality while also downplaying cultural differences so as not to scare off men (Lee and Vaught 2003). The dragon lady, lotus blossom, prostitute with a heart of gold, and the "little brown fucking machine powered by rice" (Parreñas Shimizu 2007, p. 4) are all problematic stereotypes for Asian girls. Provocatively, however, filmmaker Parreñas Shimizu sees damaging and empowering as two potentialities available in the viewing and taking in of Asian women sexualized in movies. She writes that for herself, she is both elated and tortured, and that simply viewing the Asian woman in a sexual scene creates the potential for a reading that sees her as an agent or potentially sets up a "frame of mutuality."

MEDIA IN THE SEX EDUCATION CLASSROOM

In our sexual ethics classroom, we used the music video "Bitch Bad" to inspire discussion about media, race, and sexuality. The music video for "Bitch Bad", by Lupe Fiasco (2012), both exists within the genre of hip-hop and attempts to provide a conscious critique of hip-hop. By showing this video in the "Media and Objectification" lesson of the SECS-C, (www.sexandethics.org), we hoped to challenge students to think critically about mainstream hip-hop and discuss Fiasco's comments on the genre.

The overall concept of "Bitch Bad" is how two different young people, one male, one female, encounter mainstream, "bitch"-spewing hip-hop in quite different contexts and come to different conclusions. The video opens with a White or light-skinned man counting his cash while a Black or dark-skinned man, in the position of a low-wage worker, is putting up a sign for a performance in front of a theater. Then three "acts" (verses) begin. The first act focuses on a young boy, "Shortie," who, in the lyrics has an "undeveloped context" but who listens to these rap songs with his mother in the car singing along the words, "I'm a bad bitch." As a result, the boy defines "bad bitch" in a positive way to describe an independent woman. In Act 2, a group of girls identified as "nine through twelve" watch rap videos which on the internet, Fiasco points out, come "uncensored." They are described as "malleable" and "probably unmentored." The video they watch has a man counting money and a hypersexualized women writhing against him, stroking him, and sucking on a lollipop. The lyrics point out that they don't see a paid actress, just what makes a "bad bitch" and want to imitate her to get male attention. In Act 3, teenage versions of the boy and girl meet, and the girl grown up is dressed like the women she saw sexually objectified in the rap video; but while she is sexy, she is also seen as demeaned in his eyes, a "hot mess," given he was raised by a "bad bitch"/independent woman. Fiasco lets us know that she is "really nice and smart" but caught in an illusion. This, Fiasco raps, is "the fruit of the confusion," a way in which misunderstanding about sexual norms between men and women gets perpetuated through media across generations.

The video adds another layer of social commentary when it dramatizes footage from a fictional behind-the-scenes-look at the making of the hip-hop video that the girls were watching in Act 2. In the fake rap video that played out behind the group of young girls, we see a rapper enacting gangsta rapper stereotypes while a sexualized woman writhes on him and his car. In all, there is the actual video, interspersed with short scenes of the problematic gangsta rap video, and short behind-the-scenes scenes looking at the actors putting on make-up and wigs before they make the problematic gangsta video. Later, we see them putting on blackface. When in blackface they perform a version of the stereotype of a happy Negro of old, waving their hands in white gloves. These shots are juxtaposed with authentic-appearing sadness in the faces of the performers backstage. They are also faces full of anguish or anger. Towards the end of the video, these same actors (a man and a woman) are paid by a White man. Then we witness them removing blackface make-up, suggesting that male gangsta rappers and female models/video girls are the modern day equivalent of Black blackface performers. To add another layer, there appears to be old footage of minstrel shows in the background for some of the final scenes. These shots are part of the scenes of the close-ups of the man and woman taking off their blackface, tears rolling down their faces. The very same "booty" that was emphasized in the video is used at the end of the video for a needle (either for silicone or heroin) in the final moments. And in the final lyrics, we hear a background voice ring out behind Lupe's chorus "Bitch bad, woman good, lady better, greatest motherhood" and the background voice calls out, "I'm killing these bitches." While this counterpoint phrase occurred earlier, Fiasco gives that voice the last words for the song. The last image is of a stereotyped Black cartoon character with a gun that was the medallion on the gangsta's necklace, next to possibly crack burning in an ashtray. The video is dedicated then to Paul Robeson "and the many black actors that endured the humiliating process of blackface in America."

That the two Black actors are in blackface alludes to the history where not only White performers appeared in blackface, but even Black performers were asked to perform their race and stereotype their performances in blackface. Heaggans (2009) contends that contemporary hip-hop follows the same recipe, including sexism and harmful racial stereotypes, as the minstrel shows of the nineteenth century.

> Unconscious hip-hop has become markedly minstrelsy in nature. Minstrel shows—performed heavily during the 19th century by whites in blackface—consisted of comedic skits, music, and dancing that portrayed the Black person as ignorant, misogynistic, lazy, greedy, and buffoonish. The minstrel show entertained Whites who watched actors in blackface portray stereotypic notions of Black culture. The actors earned hefty bucks for their interpretation of keepin' it real on what's going on among enslaved Black folks. Many Black male hip hop artists follow the same prescriptive misogynistic, misanthropic formula that keeps White suburbanite youth begging for more since they are the largest buyers of hip hop music (p. xi).

Other scholars have made similar critiques of contemporary mainstream hip-hop, noting the ways which it aligns with the patriarchal stances embedded in the status quo, which rap originally sought to oppose. According to Young (2008), hip-hop has lost its purpose and goal of uplifting and educating the people in favor of misogyny and "iced-out diamond rings, flashy medallions and expensive fur coats." (p. 2):

> Hip-Hop's refusal to fully acknowledge issues of rape, domestic violence, increased incarceration rates, incest, and the sexual abuse of young girls as urgently as those of police brutality, racial profiling, black male incarceration, and unemployment leaves listeners wondering is Hip-Hop the voice of the Black American youth, or the Black American male? The refusal of rap artists to address the issues that are immensely important to a large segment of the Black community leaves a sour taste in the mouths of many Hip-Hop lovers. (p. 3)

This is one side of the issue for Black theorists. But, as noted earlier, Love (2012, 2013, 2014) disagrees and says that it can be used to inspire girls in the classroom and teach critical consciousness. Another scholar offers that there are no "singular constructions of gender and sexuality in hip hop" (Roseboro 2011, p. 336).

While the teachers' intent during this lesson was to draw attention to the social landscape in which women are objectified, the students tended to focus on the individual choices of women who perform in the videos, relating those individual choices to the dual concepts of respect for oneself and acting respectable so that society will see them that way. This was akin to the theme of "personal responsibility" French (2013) found in her interviews with girls of color. Individual choice became a refrain entwined with the discourse of respectability. In one class discussion on the hip hop industry and objectification, girls continued to place blame on women in the videos for their own objectification in music videos. They used a specific construct of "classy" which we understood as similar to "respectable" to label how women should behave.

Millie: Because you see it in videos all the time, half naked girls. So obviously they don't agree. (We think she means that the women in the video don't agree that it is objectifying.)

Teacher: Yeah. And how do you think they would justify that?

Millie: I was going to say they don't agree because all the girls would stop.

Teacher: So all the girls would stop participating in the videos?

Millie: Yeah they'd stop. They'd start trying to *act classy.* They would stop trying to sell their looks and their bodies because they'd be like, oh I don't want to be a bad bitch anyway.

Similar to the participants in French's (2013) study, where their concept of empowerment remained at the personal level and often took a victim-blaming approach.

The girls distanced themselves from the girl in music videos or objectified advertisements and asserted themselves as different by judging her: "I've seen all those videos," one girl explained, "but it's not like I'm gonna be like a video girl or anything, 'cause I have more respect for myself." This statement in and of itself also evokes the liberal and perhaps neoliberal (Bay-Cheng and Eliseo-Arras 2008; Lamb and Randazzo 2016) perspective that sexism can be eradicated through individual self-projects and choices.

Shawna: At the end of the day, she shouldn't put the blame on anybody, she had a responsibility to teach her children (voices of approval). Whoever was watching those three little girls (referring to the girls in the video), they could have told them you need to get off the internet watching that thing they didn't, and the mom didn't have to let the little boy hear her saying that. It's not the person who made the video's fault because at the end of the day, the children didn't have to watch it.

In writings on Black women and respectability politics, it has been noted that Black women who enjoy hip-hop may experience some internal conflict (Love 2012; Noble 2000; Weekes 2002). In the SECS-C classrooms, the conflict was dramatized and distanced as a concern for the younger generations. Careful to avoid vulnerability of the self, girls tended to exclude themselves from anxiety over the influence of media and focus instead on siblings, constructed as more innocent and less aware of sexuality.

Amie: I'm not even going to lie, I've messed up my sister because, honestly, all I ever listened to was rap music. I have speakers in my house and I play it so all of my house can hear it. They have a song called Booty Shaking, and one day my sister came up to me and said, I wish I had boobs as big as yours. I swear I wanted to punch her because she's ten and she's thinking stuff like that...So at the end of the day, you can't blame a child for learning something. Whoever was around them should have thought about it before they put that on.

Notice the student's positioning of herself as immune to the "bad influence" although the harm to younger people is unavoidable. In another conversation, a girl says

> I feel like the generations that come up after us are going to get more affected by it because this whole situation didn't start affecting people until recently. For us it's not going to be that much of a challenge.

One male student spoke of his conflict when his nephew used the word "bitch":

Kenneth: My nephew, I listen to a good amount of rap music, so me and my sister and we saw *F'ing Problem*, and the lyrics go like "I love all my bitches." My nephew was like, a couple minutes later, he said "I love bad bitches" and we had to explain it to him, and my sister slapped him and said "don't you ever call a women bitches ever in your life!"

Kendra: That's not his fault! She shouldn't have hit him.

Kenneth: My sister's right, but then again, he's only six years old. I was trying to explain it to him, that if ever call a woman a bitch, you're going to regret it. Besides the fact that she's going to kill you, your mother's going to kill you, and I got the belt for you too.

Kendra: Black people do such a bad perception! Children getting whipped!

Kenneth: That's how we were raised, though!

Kendra was concerned about the students' representation of Black culture, and/or perhaps about the White teacher's perception of Black culture, which speaks to the overarching concern about "respectable" behavior. The boy replied that he was simply speaking the truth about how he was raised. That hip-hop may be teaching his younger brother to objectify women is a concern, but that it may be similarly affecting him is not part of his understanding. It is interesting, however, that he was called out by his classmate for representing Black culture problematically in the same way that the girls in the video were expected to represent womanhood in a better way. This idea that individuals "represent" and thus hold primary responsibility for others' stereotypes or misogyny is one that might get in the way of a closer look at institutionalized forces.

As teachers sometimes we wanted the students to acknowledge the intersection of race and gender in ways that they were either not ready to do or not willing to do with a White teacher. In one class, however, the discussion of the Black actors putting on White face in the video, introduced history that had the students rapt with outrage and intensity. In this class, it was a male African American student who claimed the position of authority and held the other students' attention while the White teacher provided additional details. After a moment in which a White teacher, Sharon, believed that some of these students were hearing about the minstrel shows for the first time and responding with shock and anger, the student who was speaking summed up minstrel shows by saying that this was in the past and it doesn't happen anymore. Sharon then tried to make the Lupe Fiasco point that perhaps Black men and women in hip-hop are being asked to perform a stereotype for a White public, the students were unwilling to pursue this tack. They were able to align themselves with the outrage of exploitation in terms of race, but returned to seeing girls who pose in videos as girls who do not respect themselves.

Tangela, an African American woman, experienced similar resistance from students during her lessons. Because she identified as a feminist, she struggled with the students' perception of feminism as wholly incompatible with hip hop culture and marginalized racial identities, even though she presented herself as someone who enjoyed hip hop and who identified as African American. In discussions about objectification, this teacher found it difficult to engage students in a discussion about the difference between making an objective choice to participate in a certain action (e.g., becoming a video vixen) and living in a society in which one is made to feel as if your choices are limited, thus elevating a video vixen lifestyle into the only viable choice of employment. Their unwillingness to acknowledge background conditions that narrowed women's choices felt not only frustrating, but at times also hurtful.

THE MEDIA LITERACY MOVEMENT

Many have called for increased media literacy. In our own project, our inclusion of the lesson on Lupe Fiasco's "Bitch Bad" is an example of the kind of media literacy that dissects problem media. In this way we support Gill's (2012) view that media itself is not the problem and may in some cases be the answer. But we take note in our own classrooms Gill's warning that being able to dissect and critique media is not any inoculation against its harmful effects, and that knowledge alone may not change hearts and attitudes. As in our own groups and the girls studied by Jackson and Vares (2015), the same girls who object to photo shopping are harmed by it. For queer or Lesbian girls, while they may use online communities to "overcome devaluation and marginalization" (Driver 2007, p. 23) they too are caught up in idealizing White, middle-class, heterosexual femininity (Brown and Thomas 2014). They write that in spite of developing sophisticated critiques, the photos still made them "feel bad" or "sad."

Gill (2012) makes another point against media literacy and that is that it is often taken up into a neoliberal project of self-improvement. Rather than changing media or the corporations producing it, the change must be in the individual who is made responsible for understanding and resisting. She asks, "When did engaging with sexist media seem to call out for an ever more sophisticated and literate media user, rather than a campaign to stamp out sexism?" (p. 742).

Her final point about media literacy is relevant to this book's project: that sexualization operates within a gendering, racializing, heteronormative, disablist economy and one can't really talk about sexualization and change without addressing these aspects. The current debate focuses so exclusively on the imagined White Western 13- or 14-year-old girl, whether named as such or not, that the intersection of sexualization with these other problems is rarely discussed.

But as we have seen, the discussion about sexy as powerful is just as present in the conversations of girls of color. It is complicated by a discourse of respect and of pride in the non-White ideals of beauty that girls of color want to honor. In this way, the "false" empowerment that sexualized media commodifies works to sell power but also sells a kind of inclusion that does in some way give visibility, if not actual power. Media can both reify and challenge stereotypes and do so simultaneously (Lindsey 2013).

CHAPTER 6

Recommendations: Working with Girls of Color Around Issues of Sexuality, Sexualization, and Sex Education

Abstract We finish the book with recommendation about how those in agencies that provide counseling or education, teachers, sex educators, and communities might respond to girls of color and their need for sex education and positive messaging about sexuality. Our recommendations address media sexualization and objectification; how sex education classes can be sensitive to the needs of girls of color; and how sex educators, parents, and others can support the complex sexual development that occurs in adolescence

Keywords Respect · Pride · Family culture · Healthy sexuality · Adolescence · Sexual violence · Critique · White Western ideals · Community

Our work began with the premise that if we, meaning parents, school personnel, feminists, counselors, sisters, and mentors, don't talk about sex with girls of color, we leave wide open a space for others to do the talking. Those who can claim public space for talking about sex still tend to be men and White and interested in making money over girls' development. While President Obama may have changed the path of sex education with his call for evidence-based programs (Obama 2009), he disappointed those of us concerned with the development of girls of color when he called for the "My Brother's Keeper" initiative (Obama 2014). We need to be our

© The Author(s) 2016
S. Lamb et al., *Girls of Color, Sexuality, and Sex Education*,
DOI 10.1057/978-1-137-60155-1_6

sisters' keepers, especially in matters of sex and sexuality where the interests of others and a long history of labeling has left scars of oppression and invades practices that wear the cloak of empowerment.

RESPECT, PRIDE, AND FAMILY CULTURES

Everyone can jump on the Respect bandwagon. Simply using the word "respect" in the classroom brought applause from students. It's a powerful word and so can be used and misused by anyone to bring people onto the same page in a moment. Everyone deserves respect. The issue in our classrooms and focus groups had to do with whether that respect has to be earned by the individual. This is where history can make a difference.

Discussions of respect and pride with girls of color should include education about the complex history that influences these terms. Girls should understand how the idea of respect has been both used strategically and later problematized, as we explained in Chap. 3. Those who work with girls need to consider disentangling the notion of respect from sexual purity, and consider how the term can be used to convey anger or even disrespect for girls as sexual beings. The implications of the term should thus be openly discussed, and girls could be asked to consider aspects of culture that influence and/or signify respect (e.g., money).

The history of pride should also be discussed with regard to more than just beauty and body image. While it is true that girls of color, like many adolescents, may start at a place of appearance in discussing pride and soon move on to the ways in which girls of color have been asked to conform to a White Western ideal, the discussion has to move beyond appearance. This would mean discussing pride in one's history, one's family, one's community, and also one's personal accomplishments. Note that we de-individualize pride by asking girls to look for pride in social places, connecting their own individual histories to these other histories.

TALKING ABOUT HEALTHY SEXUALITY

Adolescence is a time of exploration while also a time in which the culture begins to police girls' explorations. Some girls will want to explore more than others, based on their personalities and family cultures, while others may be more tentative when it comes to the topic of sex. We are not advocating that a new slew of expectations be placed on girls who want to experiment with sex, rule-breaking, and identity; there are enough media messages that they should be having a grand time partying and having sex. Rather, we want all girls to feel supported and know that a mix of feelings around sexuality is typical. It is important to affirm for girls that all people are sexual from birth. As such, having sexual feelings (or not) is a completely natural part of being human. They need to know that at times, sexual feelings may come up under odd circumstances and/or in situations in which individuals may feel as though it is not right or "natural." Through open discussion of culture, health facts, and media, we can minimize the pain and confusion such feelings can evoke. And while all feelings are acceptable, we can start a discussion about what is legal, safe, and expressive of who they are and who they want to be. While we support education that speaks of joy and pleasure, we acknowledge the world girls live in and support the idea that we also need to speak to girls about danger. It is fine enough for scholars to complain about the focus on danger in sex education, but our colleagues' research on sexual assaults and our current research on bystanders in sexual situations leads us to believe that this danger can not be ignored. Thus, it is important to emphasize physical safety in the context of relationships and sexual exploration and ground this safety in the idea of mutuality, consent, and lack of coercion. That said, although we emphasize a sexual ethics perspective in sex education, we believe that knowledge about contraception and social skills training about how to talk about contraception is also an important goal.

Another important consideration when talking about healthy sexuality is the messages that girls of color receive about what it means to be sexy. Where do these ideas about what it means to be sexy come from? Girls should know that cultural messages they receive about what men and boys think is sexy—based on TV and jokes and movies—might be very different from what real boys and men think is sexy. And if they are gay, bi, trans, or beginning to discover these sexualities or gender non-conforming identities, they should know that determinants of what is sexy are fluid, changeable, and related to communities that sometimes support Western White norms, but most of the time create new norms.

It may also be helpful to name the contradictions in expectations when girls of color are celebrated for diversity of their looks and yet are evaluated according to standards of White Western beauty. A recent Saturday Night Live sketch poked fun at this standard in "The Day Beyoncé turned Black" (Saturday Night Live 2016). Two White people discuss her new song, one saying, "Maybe this song isn't for us" and the other responds, "But usually everything is!" They then discuss her past singles arguing over whether she was Black or White in each. This was in response to a Super Bowl performance in which she was dressed as a Black Panther (on the 50th anniversary of the Black Panther Party for Self Defense), a performance that the media referred to as "unapologetic blackness" as well as courageous in speaking out against police racism (Willoughby 2016). We note this current presentation to highlight the fact that there are forms of media that resist, play with, and critique cultural norms in ways adolescents enjoy. Adolescents too, as cultural critics, typically have these same discussions that comedians and journalists have.

It is important to remember that many adolescent girls want to be sexy, like Beyoncé and other pop stars. Why would we want to shame them for this fairly typical part of development and adolescents? Being sexy and attracting attention is not altogether problematic and, as the girls told us, part of imitating stars, having fun together, fashion, and creating an image, seems far removed from any purported goal of attracting male attention. We need to counter the idea that a girl is personally responsible for any negative attention she might receive from putting on "sexy". We want girls to know that looking sexy, whether it is because they want to attract sexual attention or because they want to be fashionable, does not mean they are "asking for" negative attention. The blame should not be on them for being sexy, but rather on others' interpretations of them. And the idea that boys and men are uncontrollable is another myth that needs deconstruction in sex education classrooms.

As we noted in earlier chapters, Black girls in particular tend to be seen by White teachers and staff as more adult than White girls. In our focus groups, the girls complained about how a White girl can wear an outfit and get away with it in school, whereas a Black girl who has a more developed body will wear the same outfit and get called out for being provocative. In this way their bodies are blamed for being "too sexual." Punishments for dress and for bodies are all too common in schools and policies around dress need to be examined carefully for racist undertones and unfair practices with regard to policing girls more than boys.

WORKING WITH GIRLS AROUND MEDIA

Working with girls around media includes creating space for discussions about the influence of media, and activism. Girls may benefit from working together to discuss media, share their feelings about media images they encounter, and deconstruct stereotypes depicted in magazines, music videos, movies, and TV shows. Some of the outcomes include increased skepticism of media messages, improved media deconstruction skills, decreased perceived realism, and improved sexual health outcomes for teens. But, as Gill (2012) noted, even the most critically conscious girls are responsive to media on an emotional level. Resistance is one tactic but broadening one's viewing and allowing other influences may be another important one that shouldn't be overlooked.

Girls can be exposed to a variety of media images, outside of the mainstream depictions of what's sexy and sexual. Those working with girls around media should ask girls to bring in examples of media that challenge mainstream media: LBT media; girls in starring roles who aren't traditionally thin, White, and blonde; and YouTube shows like *Awkward Black Girl* (Rae 2016) (which has now has become a tv show) that depict a more typical experience of growing up as a girl of color. Some videos have sex positive and progressive messages about gender relations, violence, and sex. Incorporating media literacy in general into sex education has the potential to positively influence decisions about sex (Scull et al. 2014).

That being said, we think it's important not to push our ideals of feminist perfection onto the girls with whom we work, but rather give space for the complicated issues that arise from wanting to be attractive and also wanting to conform and get praise for that. The powerful influence of the media needs to be normalized, and girls should be reminded that nothing is "wrong" with them if they, like all of us, are taken in by problematic media.

We also advocate for programming and counseling that teaches girls to be allies to each other. As Brown (2003, 2016) and Lamb and Brown (2006) pointed out, there is all too much in modern society that pushes girls against each other, sets some up as "mean girls" and others as "Queen Bees," which serves only to reinforce girls themselves as the problem, rather than the culture. Given a culture that pits girls against each other, we need to help girls to challenge each other and others when they "type" girls– that is, label each other as certain types. If we do this and see where in the media they are getting these "types," we will go far in creating a safe space in schools to be a girl.

Although media education is important, more action is needed to "move beyond the protectionist approach of the media literacy movement" (Kearney 2006, p. 109). Girl-centered media education programs can critically engage girls in challenging oppression by creating their own media as in HOTGIRLS, Inc. (Helping Our Teen Girls in Real Life Situations), a nonprofit in Atlanta, Georgia (Kearney 2006). Lyn Mikel Brown works with a diverse collection of girl activists in girl-fueled projects like Powered By Girl and SPARK Movement. Powered By Girl (http://poweredbygirl.org/) is an online magazine "for girls by girls" that tackles media sexism of all kinds. SPARK's website states that "SPARK Movement is a girl-fueled, intergenerational activist organization working online to ignite an anti-racist gender justice movement." Since 2010, girls on the SPARK team have ignited on the ground actions and critiqued and produced media (Edell et al. 2013). A sample of a recent blog is entitled, "The Best Little (Queer Brown) Girl in the World" and another is "Reimagining School Dress Codes." Digital media is an important space for marginalized Queer girls. Queer girls have a unique way of critically engaging with media images that plays with and transforms the intended meanings. Clearly, girls can both delight and critique media in a variety of circumstances (Jackson et al. 2012).

How can we encourage such trends? School strategies might be to identify and consult with girls who demonstrate resistance to oppressive cultural scenarios and utilize them as peer educators as SPARK does. These programs should demonstrate respect by (1) collaborating with girls; (2) building on the empowering aspects of youth culture; (3) including girls of diverse ethnicities, race, and religion; and (4) recognizing girls as knowledgeable about the role of media in their lives.

Ward et al. (2006) composed a wish list for positive media trends they hoped to see continue it the future. Our use of the Lupe Fiasco video for "Bitch Bad" embodies two of the wishes on this list, namely:

1. *An acknowledgment of gender roles and their constraints on sexuality.* Many portrayals, especially in music videos, treat the sexual double standard as natural and accepted. But traditional gender roles are often quite restrictive. We would like to see portrayals of women and men grappling with these constraints, and perhaps defying them ...

2. *Portrayals of the ambiguities and negotiations that are involved in navigating sexual relationships.* Sexuality is a journey. Each woman needs to negotiate and discover what works for her, and this answer may vary from partner to partner. We would like to see women (and men) grappling with these ambiguities. (Ward et al. 2006, p. 67)

And while we celebrate girls' involvement in media, it is important to remember, as Stokes (2007) found that girls' media can also reflect the racism, misogyny, patriarchy, and capitalism in American culture. On this topic, Thomas (2011) and Brown and Thomas (2014) argue that we need to be careful of an individualizing discourse that puts resistance into the hands of individual girls, citing that while "many girls have self-consciously become effective agents of postfeminism, often eagerly consuming the ideals of individualized self-creation and agential voice, their narratives and online practices tell a more complex story." These Queer girls situate their identities within normative heterosexual, middle class, White adolescence in their online discussions. Rather than only being seen as heroes of resistance, they reproduce the kind of subjectivity that feminism hopes to challenge.

The alternative of not involving girls is problematic too. Those adults working with girls simply have to understand that encouraging critique and solidarity around feminist issues cannot be the only aim and can itself turn into relegitimating regressive ideas of what girlhood is all about (McRobbie 2009). The most promising strategies for transforming denigrating representations of Black and other marginalized groups' female sexuality is to eliminate the pervasive social inequalities that perpetuate the oppression of minority women and girls.

Sexual Violence in the Lives of Girls of Color

In this book, we adopted a strengths-based perspective. As such, we did not discuss or present research on sexual abuse, coercion, and rape in the lives of girls of color. That being said, we consider these to be extremely important issues that were beyond the scope of this book. It is critical to note that girls of color are not free to explore and develop their sexuality in whatever forms are available if they are coping with the trauma of victimization. This should always be kept in mind, as should a recognition of racial microaggressions that can beat a girl down, and major racist events (see BlackLives Matter. com) that shape their feelings of safety in the world.

On the other hand, when a group, such as American Indian adolescent girls, is always and only researched in terms of their risks and safety, whether or not the aim is a good one, as fighting the commercial sexual exploitation of American Indian girls (Pierce 2009, 2012), we problematically define sexual health only in opposition to abuse. That there is no literature on the positive sexual development of Native American/Indigenous girls in the US speaks volumes about this country. A major concern that arises from our studies is the extent to which adolescents can shift their focus from individual women being independent and thus culpable actors in sexually violent situations to discussions of responses and solutions that can be enacted at the community level. Unfortunately, the general research literature does not provide much information or many solutions for interventions aimed at altering perceptions and/or reducing and responding to sexual violence among African American adolescents.

There are, however, some promising examples of communities and educational settings where adults and adolescents are addressing these issues. As reported in the *Chicago Tribune* (Trice 2004), in a north side neighborhood of Chicago, several African American and Caribbean girls and women reported sexually harassing "catcalls" and unwanted, aggressive touching. They felt threatened and powerless yet reported this at a youth forum. Two adolescents were then supported by the leaders of this forum to develop the Rogers Park Young Women's Action Team, which then became six adolescents who took pictures of gangways, alleys, and businesses that they determined were hot spots, put together a report they presented to the police, elected officials, and their community members. They requested better police patrols and street lighting and created a workshop on how to confront harassing men.

This example of community organization and response to violence is important because it represents several important shifts from what is represented in the data we present: (1) girls were able to move from a focus on individual women's behavior to collective behavior and shared experiences; (2) girls created new tools to understand and contextualize their experiences; (3) girls taught each other new ways to respond to dangerous situations other than avoidance; and (4) girls made demands on existing social institutions to address girls' concerns.

The above example includes many of the recommendations suggested by Freudenberg et al. (1999) in their study of the role of violence among adolescents in the South Bronx community of New York City. The authors asserted that public health professionals focus on specific risk and protective factors identified by young people in a given community and offer programs that develop meaningful relationships between youth and adults and contacts in the wider world. These recommendations, along with others demonstrate that collective action can be used as a tool to reduce sexual violence and help female adolescents think differently about their own responsibility versus the community's.

The report, Black Girls Matter (Crenshaw et al. 2015) has a number of suggestions for the improvement of schools rather than the improvement of girls themselves. Some of these include doing away with zero-tolerance policies and working toward creating safe and welcoming school environments that create a sense of belonging. Restorative rather than punitive justice needs to be the norm. Schools also need better ways of detecting trauma, sexual victimization, and interpersonal violence in the lives of Black girls to combat victimization and to understand some of the sources of "acting out" behavior.

CALL FOR RESEARCH

In the extant literature, most girls of color have been treated as subjects in need of protection from STIs and pregnancy. And, if you can find literature on under-researched minorities, it is often about statistics regarding first sex, pregnancy, and contraception use. In rare cases, research with girls of color takes place in the form of focus groups. But this is hard to do because girls don't live in totally racially uniform communities. Many of the articles we read in mainstream journals appeared to be the results of dissertations, thus making it clear that the way girls of color get into the literature is when a doctoral student decides to research them, and not through major funded initiatives. While journals have put out calls for papers showing the value of this research, there needs to be initial funding in which divisions or special interest groups fund intersectional research on girls of color. Associations like the the American Psychological Association (APA), the American Educational Research Association (AERA), or the American Sociological Association (ASA) need to support research on girls of color more clearly. The report, Black Girls Matter (Crenshaw et al. 2015) has a number of suggestions for changes that would be wise to heed.

In this book, we have cited a good deal of research that has focused on Black girls, with the realization that we need much more research on underrepresented minority girls like indigenous/Native/Native Alaskan, East Asian American, Southeast Asian American, Arab American, Muslim, Christian, and girls who have immigrated from these and other countries. We are also aware that we are in the midst of a change regarding racial identity politics such that who people are and whom they identify with is much more complex. It may be difficult to bring together girls of similar identities when they themselves see themselves as integrating multiple identities. Researchers need new ways to incorporate intersecting identities into their practice.

That said, it appears to us that we are in particular need of research on sex and sexuality of Native/Native Alaskan/Indigenous girls. And there is very little psychological research on the sexual development of Asian American and in particular South East Asian girls. The intersection of immigrant girls who enter this country and who negotiate family culture in light of school culture and media is an important area. As sexuality researchers continue to focus on college populations, they do a great disservice to the many developing girls out there whose voices could be heard in qualitative research and whose positions could be counted in quantitative research. We hope that this book will open up new areas for research with girls on girlhood and intersecting identities, and new collaborations with adults who care.

REFERENCES

Allen, L. (2007). "Pleasurable pedagogy": Young people's ideas about teaching "pleasure" in sexuality education. *21st Century Society*, *2*, 249–264.

Allen, L. (2008). "They think you shouldn't be having sex anyway": Young people's suggestions for improving sexuality education content. *Sexualities*, *11*(5), 573–594.

Alleyne, S.I., & LaPoint, V. (2004). Obesity among black adolescent girls: Genetic, psychosocial, and cultural influences. *Journal of Black Psychology*, *30*(3), 344–365. doi:10.1177/0095798404266062.

American Psychological Association, Task Force on the Sexualization of Girls (2007). *Report of the APA task force on the sexualization of girls*. Washington, DC: American Psychological Association. http://www.apa.org/pi/wpo/sexualization.html.

Arganbright, M., & Lee, M. (2007). Effects of hip-hop music video exposure on the sexual attitudes of young adults. *Conference Papers – International Communication Association 1*.

Arrizón, A. (2008). Latina subjectivity, sexuality and sensuality. *Women & Performance: A Journal of Feminist Theory*, *18*(3), 189–198.

Aubrey, J.S., Hopper, K.M., & Mbure, W.G. (2011). Check that body! The effects of sexually objectifying music videos on college men's sexual beliefs. *Journal of Broadcasting & Electronic Media*, *55*(3), 360–379.

Awad, G.H., Norwood, C., Taylor, D.S., Martinez, M., McClain, S., Jones, B., & Chapman-Hilliard, C. (2015). Beauty and body image concerns among African American college women. *Journal of Black Psychology*, *41*(6), 540–564.

Batchelor, D.C. (2006). Vulnerable voices: An examination of the concept of vulnerability in relation to student voice. *Educational Philosophy & Theory*, *38*(6), 787–800. doi:10.1111/j.1469-5812.2006.00231.x.

© The Author(s) 2016   77
S. Lamb et al., *Girls of Color, Sexuality, and Sex Education*,
DOI 10.1057/978-1-137-60155-1

Bay-Cheng, L.Y. (2012). Recovering empowerment: De-personalizing and re-politicizing adolescent female sexuality. *Sex Roles*, *66*(11–12), 713–717. doi:10.1007/s11199-011-0070-x.

Bay-Cheng, L.Y. & Eliseo-Arras, R.K. (2008). The making of unwanted sex: Gendered and neoliberal norms in college women's unwanted sexual experiences. *Journal of Sex Research*, *45*, 386–397.

Blum, L. (2012). Moral asymmetry: A problem for the protected categories approach. *Lewis and Clark Law Review*, *16*(2), 101–109.

Botta, R.A. (2003). For your health? The relationship between magazine reading and adolescents' body image and eating disturbances. *Sex Roles*, *48*(9–10), 389–399.

Boyd, E.M., Reynolds, J.R., Tillman, K.H., & Martin, P.Y. (2011). Adolescent girls' race/ethnic status, identities, and drive for thinness. *Social Science Research*, *40*(2), 667–684. doi:http://dx.doi.org.proxy.lib.umich.edu/10.1016/j.ssresearch.2010.11.003

Brown, L.M. (2003). *Girlfighting betrayal and rejection among girls*. New York: New York University Press.

Brown, L.M. (2016). *Powered by girl: A field guide for working with girl activists*. Boston: Beacon Press.

Brown, A. & Thomas, M.E. (2014). "I just like knowing they can look at it and realize who I really am": Recognition and the limits of girlhood agency on MySpace. *Signs: Journal of Women in Culture and Society*, *39*(4), 949–972.

Brown, J.D., K.L. L'Engle, C.J. Pardun, G. Guang, K. Kenneavy, and C. Jackson. (2006). Sexy media matter: Exposure to sexual content in music, movies, television, and magazines predicts black and white adolescents' sexual behavior. *Pediatrics*, *117*(4), 1018–1027. doi:10.1542/peds.2005-1406.

Bucchianeri, M.M., Fernandes, N., Loth, K., Hannan, P.J., Eisenberg, M.E., & Neumark-Sztainer, D. (2016). Body dissatisfaction: do associations with disordered eating and psychological well-being differ across race/ethnicity in adolescent girls and boys? *Cultural Diversity and Ethnic Minority Psychology*, *22*(1), 137–146.

Capodilupo, C.M. (2015). One size does not fit all: Using variables other than the thin deal to understand Black women's body image. *Cultural Diversity and Ethnic Minority Psychology*, *21*(2), 268–278.

Capodilupo, C.M., & Kim, S. (2014). Gender and race matter: The importance of considering intersections in Black women's body image. *Journal of Counseling Psychology*, *61*(1), 37–41. doi:http://dx.doi.org/10.1037/a0034597.

Carlson, S.J. (1992). Black ideals of womanhood in the late Victorian era. *The Journal of Negro History*, *77*(2), 61–73.

Carroll, N. (2000). Ethnicity, race, and monstrosity: The rhetorics of horror and humor. In P.Z. Brand (Ed.), *Beauty matters* (37–56). Bloomington, IN: Indiana University Press.

Chithambo, T.P., & Huey, S.J. (2013). Black/white differences in perceived weight and attractiveness among overweight women. *Journal of Obesity, 2013*, 1–4. doi:http://dx.doi.org/10.1155/2013/320326.

Chou, R. (2012). *Asian American sexual politics: The construction of race, gender, and sexuality*. Lanham, MD: Rowman & Littlefield.

Collins, P.H. (1990). *Black feminist thought: Knowledge, consciousness, and the politics of empowerment*. Boston: Unwin Hyman.

Collins, P.H. (2000). *Black feminist thought: Knowledge, consciousness, and the politics of empowerment*. New York: Routledge.

Collins, P.H. (2004). *Black sexual politics: African Americans, gender, and the new racism*. New York: Routledge.

Cooper, C.M. (2007). Worrying about vaginas: Feminism and Eve Ensler's *The Vagina Monologues*. *Signs, 32*(3), 727–758.

Cooper, K.J. (2015). Black girls matter. *Diverse Issues in Higher Education, 32*(4), 16–17.

Coy, M. (2009). Milkshakes, lady lumps and growing up to want boobies: How the sexualization of popular culture limits girls' horizons. *Child Abuse Review, 18*(6), 372–383.

Crenshaw, K., Ocen, P., & Nanda, J. (2015). Black girls matter: Pushed out, overpoliced and underprotected. Report issued by the African American Policy Forum (AAPF) and Columbia Law School's Center for Intersectionality and Social Policy Studies.

DiClemente, R.J., Wingood, G.M., Crosby, R., Cobb, B.K., Harrington, K., & Davies, S.L. (2001). Parent-adolescent communication and sexual risk behaviors among African American adolescent females. *The Journal of Pediatrics, 139*, 407–412.

Demarest, J., & Allen, R. (2000). Body image: gender, ethnic, and age differences. *The Journal of Social Psychology, 140*(4), 465–472.

Dines, G. (2010). *Pornland: How porn has hijacked our sexuality*. Boston: Beacon Press.

Driver, S. (2007). *Queer girls and popular culture: Reading, resisting, and creating Media*. New York: Lang.

Du Bois, W.E.B. (1903). *The souls of black folk*. Chicago: A.C. McClurg & Co.

Duckworth, A. (2016). *Grit: The power of passion and perseverance*. New York: Scribner.

Duke, L. (2000). Black in a blonde world: Race and girls' interpretations of the feminine ideal in teen magazines. *Journalism & Mass Communication Quarterly, 77*(2), 367–392.

Duncan, G.A. (2005). Black youth, identity, and ethics. *Educational Theory*, *55*, 3–22.

Durham, M. G. (2004). Constructing the "new ethnicities": Media, sexuality and diaspora identity in the lives of South Asian immigrant girls. *Critical Studies in Media Communication*, *21*(2), 140–161.

Dyson, M.E. (2014, November 30). Where do we go after Ferguson? *The New York Times*, pp. SR1.

Edell, D., Brown, L.M., & Tolman, D. (2013). Embodying sexualization: When theory meets practice in intergenerational feminist activism. *Feminist Theory*, *14*(3), 275–284.

Egan, R.D., and Hawkes, G.L. (2008). Endangered girls and incendiary objects: Unpacking the discourse on sexualization. *Sexuality & Culture*, *12*(4), 291–311. doi:10.1007/s12119-008-9036-8.

Ensler, E. (1998). *The vagina monologues*. New York: Villard.

Erikson, E.H. (1966). Eight ages of man. *International Journal of Psychiatry*, *2*, 281–307.

Espiritu, Y.L. (2001). "We don't sleep around like white girls do": Family, culture, and gender in Filipina American lives. *Signs*, *26*(2), 415–440.

Everett, K.B. (2000). Latina identity and the perils of femininity. http://oak trust.library.tamu.edu/handle/1969.1/ETD-TAMU-2000-FELLOWS-THESIS-E96.

Falconer, J.W., & Neville, H.A. (2000). African American college women's body image: An examination of body mass, African self-consciousness, and skin color satisfaction. *Psychology of Women Quarterly*, *24*, 236–243.

Ferguson, A. (2001). *Bad boys: Public schools in the making of black masculinity*. Ann Arbor, MI: University of Michigan Press.

Ferguson, C.J., Muñoz, M.E., Garza, A., & Galindo, M. (2014). Concurrent and prospective analyses of peer, television and social media influences on body dissatisfaction, eating disorder symptoms and life satisfaction in adolescent girls. *Journal of Youth and Adolescence*, *43*(1), 1–14.

Fiasco, L. (2012). "Bitch Bad" [Music Video]. https://www.youtube.com/watch?v=C3m3t_PxiUI.

Fields, J. (2005). "Children having children": Race, innocence, and sexuality education. *Social Problems*, *52*(4): 549–71.

Fields, J. (2008). *Risky lessons: Sex education and social inequality*. New Brunswick, NJ: Rutgers University Press.

Fine, M. (1988). Sexuality, schooling, and adolescent females: The missing discourse of desire. *Harvard Educational Review*, *58*(1), 29–53.

Fine, M., and S.I. McClelland. (2006). Sexuality education and the discourse of desire: Still missing after all these years. *Harvard Educational Review*, *76*, 297–338.

Fitzsimmons-Craft, E.E., & Bardone-Cone, A.M. (2012). Examining prospective mediation models of body surveillance, trait anxiety, and body dissatisfaction in African American and Caucasian college women. *Sex Roles*, *67*(3–4), 187–200.

Fletcher, K.D., Ward, L.M., Thomas, K., Foust, M., Levin, D., & Trinh, S. (2015). Will it help? Identifying socialization discourses that promote sexual risk and sexual health among African American youth. *The Journal of Sex Research*, *52*(2), 199–212.

Franiuk, R., Seefelt, J., & Vandello, J. (2008). Prevalence of rape myths in headlines and their effects on attitudes toward rape. *Sex Roles*, *58*(11–12), 790–801.

Fredrickson, B.L., & Roberts, T. (1997). Objectification theory: Toward understanding women's lived experiences and mental health risks. *Psychology of Women Quarterly*, *21*, 173–206. doi:10.1111/j.1471-6402.1997.tb00108.x.

French, B. (2013). More than Jezebels and Freaks: Exploring how black girls navigate sexual coercion and sexual scripts. *Journal of African American Studies*, *17*(1), 39–50.

Freud, A. (1936/1993). *The ego and the mechanisms of defense*. London: Karnac Books.

Freudenberg, N., Roberts, L., Richie, B.E., Taylor, R.T., McGillicuddy, K., & Greene, M.B. (1999). Coming up in the boogie down: The role of violence in the lives of adolescents in the South Bronx. *Health Education & Behavior*, *26*(6), 788–805.

Frisby, C.M. (2004). Does race matter? Effects of idealized images on African American women's perceptions of body esteem. *Journal of Black Studies*, *34*(3), 323–347.

Froyum, C.M. (2010). Making "good girls": Sexual agency in the sexuality education of low income black girls. *Culture, Health & Sexuality*, *12*(1), 59–82.

Garcia, L. (2009). "Now why do you want to know about that?": Heteronormativity, sexism, and racism in the sexual (mis)education of Latina youth. *Gender & Society*, *23*, 520–541.

García, L., & Torres, L. (2009). New directions in Latina sexualities studies. *NWSA Journal*, *21*(3), vii–xvi.

Garrod, A.C., Smulyan, L., Powers, S.I., & Kilkenny, R. (2005). *Adolescent portraits: Identity, relationships, and challenges* (5th ed.). Auckland: Pearson Education.

Gill, R.C. (2007). Critical respect: The difficulties and dilemmas of agency and "choice" for feminism: A reply to Duits and van Zoonen. *European Journal of Women's Studies Journal*, *14*(1), 69–80.

Gill, R. (2012). Media, empowerment and the 'sexualization of culture' debates. *Sex Roles*, *66*(11–12), 736–745. doi:10.1007/s11199-011-0107-1.

Gordon, K.H., Castro, Y., Sitnikov, L., & Holm-Denoma, J.M. (2010). Cultural body shape ideals and eating disorder symptoms among White, Latina, and Black college women. *Cultural Diversity and Ethnic Minority Psychology*, *16*(2), 135–143. doi:http://dx.doi.org/10.1037/a0018671.

Grabe, S., & Hyde, J.S. (2009). Body objectification, MTV, and psychological outcomes among female adolescents. *Journal of Applied Social Psychology*, *39*(12), 2840–2858.

Greenwood, D.N., & Dal Cin, S. (2012). Ethnicity and body consciousness: Black and White American women's negotiation of media ideals and others' approval. *Psychology of Popular Media Culture*, *1*(4), 220–235.

Gunter, B. (2012). The role of the media. In Rumsey, N. & Harcourt, D. (Eds.), *The Oxford handbook of the psychology of appearance* (455–467). New York: Oxford University Press.

Guzmán, B., Arruda, E., & Feria, A. (2006). Los papas, la familia, y la sexualidad. In J. Denner & B. Guzmán (Eds.), *Latina girls: Voices of adolescent strength in the United States* (17–28). New York: NYU Press.

Hahm, H.C., Lahiff, M., & Baretto, R.M. (2006). Asian American adolescents' first sexual intercourse: Gender and acculturation differences. *Perspectives on Sexual and Reproductive Health*, *38*(1), 28–36.

Hald, G., Malamuth, N.M., & Yuen, C. (2010). Pornography and attitudes supporting violence against women: Revisiting the relationship in nonexperimental studies. *Aggressive Behavior*, *36*(1), 14–20.

Halliwell, E., & Diedrichs, P.C. (2012). Influence of the media. In Rumsey, N. & Harcourt, D. (Eds.), *The Oxford handbook of the psychology of appearance* (217–238). New York: Oxford University Press.

Harris, P. (2003). Gatekeeping and remaking: The politics of respectability in African American women's history and Black feminism. *Journal of Women's History*, *15*(1), 212–220.

Harris, F. (2014). The rise of respectability politics. *Dissent*. https://www.dissent magazine.org/article/the-rise-of-respectability-politics.

Harris-Perry, M.V. (2011). *Sister citizen: Shame, stereotypes, and black women in America*. New Haven, CT: University Press.

Heaggans, Raphael (Author). (2009). *The 21st century hip-hop minstrel show: Are we continuing the blackface tradition?* San Diego, CA: University Readers.

Henderson, C.D. (2014). Sarah Baartman: The Hottentot Venus, and Black women's identity. *Women's Studies*, *43*(7), 946–959.

Henwood, K. (2008). Qualitative research, reflexivity and living with risk: Valuing and practicing epistemic reflexivity and centering marginality. *Qualitative Research in Psychology*, *5*(1), 45–55. doi:10.1080/14780880701863575.

Hernandez, J. (2009). Miss, You Look Like a Bratz Doll": On Chonga Girls and Sexual-Aesthetic Excess. *NWSA Journal*, *21*(3), 63–90.

Hesse-Biber, S.N., Howling, S.A., Leavy, P., & Lovejoy, M. (2004). Racial identity and the development of body image issues among African American adolescent girls. *The Qualitative Report*, *9*, 49–79.

Hetherington, C., Burleson, T., & Millitello, C. (2007). Issues in Latina sexual health. http://www.umich.edu/~ac213/student_projects07/latinahealth/sexualhealth.html.

Higginbotham, E.B. (1992). African-American women's history and the metalanguage of race. *Signs: Journal of Women in Culture* & *Society, 17*(2), 251–274.

Higginbotham, E., & Weber, L. (1992). Moving up with kin and community: Upward social mobility for Black and White women. *Gender & Society, 6*(3): 416–440. doi:10.1177/089124392006003005.

Hill, M.E. (2002). Skin color and the perception of attractiveness among African Americans: Does gender make a difference? *Social Psychology Quarterly, 65*, 77–91.

Hunter, M.L. (2002). "If you're light you're alright": Light skin color as social capital for women of color. *Gender & Society, 16*, 175–193.

Iglesias, E., & Cormier, S. (2002). The transformation of girls to women: Finding voice and developing strategies for liberation. *Journal of Multicultural Counseling and Development, 30*, 259–271.

Irvine, J. (2002). *Talk about sex: The battles over sex education in the United States.* Berkeley, CA: University of California Press.

Isom, D. (2012). Fluid and shifting: Racialized, gendered, and sexual identity in African American children. *The International Journal of Interdisciplinary Social Sciences, 6*(11), 127–137.

Jackson, S. & Vares, T. (2015). "Too many bad role models for us girls": Girls, female pop celebrities and sexualization. *Sexualities, 18*(4), 480–498.

Jackson, S., Vares, T., & Gill, R. (2012). "The whole playboy mansion image": Girls' fashioning and fashioned selves within a postfeminist culture. *Feminism & Psychology, 23*(2), 143–162.

Javier, S.J., & Belgrave, F.Z. (2015). An examination of influences on body dissatisfaction among Asian American college females: Do family, media, or peers play a role? *Journal of American College Health, 63*(8), 579–583. doi:10.1080/07448481.2015.1031240.

Jhally, S., Killoy, A., Bartone, J., & Media Education Foundation. (2007). *Dreamworlds 3: Desire, sex & power in music video.* Northampton, MA: Media Education Foundation.

Jimenez, J.A., & Abreu, J. (2003). Race and sex effects on attitudinal perceptions of acquaintance rape. *Journal of Counseling Psychology, 50*(2), 252–256. doi:10.1037/0022-0167.50.2.252.

Jones, E. (2013). On the real: Agency, abuse, and sexualized violence in Rihanna's "Russian Roulette". *African American Review, 46*(Spring), 71–86.

Juárez, A.M., & Kerl, S.B. (2003). What is the right (white) way to be sexual? Reconceptualizing Latina sexuality. *Aztlan: A Journal of Chicano Studies, 28*(1), 5–37.

Kearney, M.C. (2006). *Girls make media*. New York: Routledge.

Kelch-Oliver, K., & Ancis, J.R. (2011). Black women's body image: An analysis of culture-specific influences. *Women & Therapy*, *34*(4), 345–358.

Kennedy, R. (2015). Lifting as we climb. *Harper's Magazine*. https://harpers.org/archive/2015/10/lifting-as-we-climb/.

Lamb, S. (2002). *The secret lives of girls: What good girls really do, sex play, aggression, and their guilt*. New York: Free Press.

Lamb, S. (2006). *Sex, therapy, and kids: Addressing their concerns through talk and play*. New York: W. W. Norton & Co.

Lamb, S. (2013a). The future of sex education: Just the facts? *Educational Theory*, *63*(5), 443–460.

Lamb, S. (2013b). *Sex education for a caring society: Creating an ethics-based curriculum*. New York: Teachers College Press.

Lamb, S., & Brown, L.M. (2006). *Packaging girlhood: Rescuing our daughters from marketers' schemes*. New York: St. Martin's Press.

Lamb, S., & Plocha, A. (2015). Pride and sexiness: Girls of color discuss race, body image, and sexualization. *Girlhood Studies*, *8*(2), 86–102. doi:10.3167/ghs.2015.080207.

Lamb, S., & Randazzo, R. (2016). From I to we: Sex education as a form of civics education in a neoliberal context. *Curriculum Inquiry*, *46*(2), 148–167. doi.org/10.1080/03626784.2016.1144465.

Lamb, S., Farmer, K., Kosterina, E., Lambe Sariñana, S., Plocha, A., & Randazzo, R. (2016). What's sexy? What's sexualization? Confidence, rebellion, and trying too hard. In *Gender and Education*, *28*(4), 527–545. doi.org/10.1080/09540253.2015.1107528

Latner, J.D., Knight, T., & Illingworth, K. (2011). Body image and self-esteem among Asian, Pacific Islander, and White college students in Hawaii and Australia. *Eating Disorders*, *19*(4), 355–368. doi:10.1080/10640266.2011.584813.

Lee, S. (2010). *Erotic revolutionaries: Black women, sexuality, and popular culture*. Falls Village, CT: Hamilton Books.

Lee, L., & Goodman, J. (2010). Romantic love, sexuality, and popular culture: A study of young Korean immigrants' perspectives. *Education and Society*, *28*(1), 25–47.

Lee, S.J., & Vaught, S. (2003). "You can never be too rich or too thin": Popular and consumer culture and the Americanization of Asian American girls and young women. *The Journal of Negro Education*, *72*(4), 457–466.

Lerum, K., & Dworkin, S. (2009). An interdisciplinary commentary on the report of the APA task force on the sexualization of girls. *Journal of Sex Research*, *46*, 250–263. doi:10.1080/00224490903079542.

Lesko, N. (2012). *Act your age: A cultural construction of adolescence*. New York: Routledge.

Lindsey, T.B. (2013). "One time for my girls": African-American girlhood, empowerment, and popular visual culture. *Journal of African American Studies*, *17*, 22–34.

Lorde, A. (1978). *Uses of the erotic: The erotic as power.* Brooklyn, NY: Out & Out Books.

Love, B.L. (2012). *Hip hop's li'l sistas speak: Negotiating identities and politics in the new south.* New York: Peter Lang.

Love, B.L. (2013). Black girlhood, embodied knowledge, and hip hop feminist pedagogy. In C. Dillard & C. Okpalaoka (Eds.), *Engaging culture, race, and spirituality in education: New visions* (167–173). New York: Peter Lang.

Love, B.L. (2014). Culturally relevant cyphers: Rethinking classroom management through hip hop-based education. In A. Honigsfeld & A. Cohan (Eds.), *Breaking the mold for culturally and linguistically diverse students: Innovative and successful practices for the 21st century* (103–110). Lanham, MD: Rowman and Littlefield.

Lui, M.T.Y. (2009). Saving young girls from Chinatown: White slavery and woman suffrage, 1910–1920. *Journal of the History of Sexuality, 18*(3), 394–403. doi:10.5555/jhs.2009.18.3.393.

Martino, S.C, Collins, R.L., Elliott, M.N., Strachman, A., Kanouse, D.E., & Berry, S.H. (2006). Exposure to degrading versus nondegrading music lyrics and sexual behavior among youth. *Pediatrics, 118*(2), e430–e441.

McCree, D.H., Wingood, G.M., DiClemente, R., Davies, S., & Harrington, K.F. (2003). Religiosity and risky sexual behavior in African-American adolescent females. *Journal of Adolescent Health, 33,* 2–8. doi:http://dx.doi.org/10.1016/S1054-139X(02)00460-3.

McRobbie, A. (2009). *The aftermath of feminism: Gender, culture, and social change.* Los Angeles: Sage.

Miller-Young, M. (2010). Putting hypersexuality to work: Black women and illicit eroticism in pornography. *Sexualities, 13*(2), 219–235.

Mitchell, S.A., & Black, M.J. (1995). *Freud and beyond: A history of modern psychoanalytic thought.* New York: Basic Books.

Morgan, J. (1995). Fly-girls, bitches and hoes: Notes of a hip-hop feminist." *Social Text 45*(Winter), pp. 151–157.

Morgan, J. (2000). *When chickenheads come to roost: A hip-hop feminist breaks it down.* New York: Simon & Schuster.

Mowatt, R.A., French, B.H., & Malebranche, D.A. (2013). Black/female/body hypervisibility and invisibility: A Black feminist augmentation of feminist leisure research. *Journal of Leisure Research, 45*(5), 644–660.

Moynihan, D.P. (1997). The Negro Family: The Case for National Action (1965). African American Male Research.

Mundorf, N., Allen, M., D'Alession, D., Emmers-Sommer, T.M. (2007). Effects of sexually explicit media. In R. Preiss, B.M. Gayle, Burrell, N., Allen, M., & Bryant, J. (Eds.), *Mass media effects research: Advances through meta-analysis.* Mahwah, NJ: Lawrence Erlbaum.

Murnen, S.K., & Don, B.P. (2012). Body image and gender roles. *Encyclopedia of Body Image and Human Appearance, 1,* 128–134.

Murnen, S.K., & Smolak, L. (2012). Social considerations related to adolescent girls' sexual empowerment: A response to Lamb and Peterson. *Sex Roles*, 66(11–12), 725–735.

Naber, N. (2006). Arab American femininities: Beyond Arab virgin/American(ized) whore. *Feminist Studies*, 32(1), 87–111.

Noble, D. (2000). Ragga music: Dis/respecting Black women and dis/resreputable sexualities. In B. Hesse (Ed.), *Unsettled multiculturalisms: Diasporas, entanglements, transruptions* (148–169). London: Zed Books.

Obama, B. (2009). Inaugural address. In J.T. Woolley & G. Peters (Ed.), *The American presidency project*. http://www.presidency.ucsb.edu/ws/index.php?pid=44.

Obama, B. (2014). My Brother's Keeper. https://www.whitehouse.gov/my-brothers-keeper.

Okazaki, S. (2002). Influences of culture on Asian Americans' sexuality. *Journal of Sex Research*, 39(1), 34–41.

Park, P. (2014). The madame butterfly effect. *Bitch Magazine: Feminist Response to Pop Culture*, 64, 28–33.

Parreñas Shimizu, C. (2005). The bind of representation: Performing and consuming hypersexualization in *Miss Saigon*. *Theatre Journal*, 57(2), 247–265.

Parreñas Shimizu, C. (2007). *The hypersexuality of race: Performing Asian/American women on screen and scene*. Durham, NC: Duke University Press.

Pascoe, C.J. (2007). *Dude, you're a fag: Masculinity and sexuality in high school*. Berkeley, CA: University of California Press.

Payne, E. (2010). Sluts: Heteronormative policing in the stories of lesbian youth. *Educational Studies*, 46, 317–336.

Payne, D.L., Lonsway, K.A., & Fitzgerald, L.F. (1999). Rape myth acceptance: Exploration of its structure and its measurement using the Illinois Rape Myth Acceptance Scale. *Journal of Research in Personality*, 33(1), 27–68.

Perkin, J. (1995). *Victorian Women*. New York: NYU Press.

Pierce, A. (2009). *Shattered hearts: The commercial sexual exploitation of American Indian women and girls in Minnesota*. Minneapolis, MN: Minnesota Indian Women's Resource Center.

Pierce, A. (2012). American Indian adolescent girls: Vulnerability to sex trafficking, Intervention strategies. *American Indian Alaskan Native Mental Health Research*, 19(1), 37–56. doi:10.5820/aian.1901.2012.37.

Plybon, L.E., Holmer, H., Hunter, A., Sheffield, C., Stephens, C., & Cavolo, L. (2009). The impact of body image and Afrocentric appearance on sexual refusal self-efficacy in early adolescent African American girls. *Sex Education*, 9(4), 437–448. doi:10.1080/14681810903265360.

Pope, M., Corona, R., & Belgrave, F.Z. (2014). Nobody's perfect: A qualitative examination of African American maternal caregivers' and their adolescent girls' perceptions of body image. *Body Image*, 11(3), 307–317.

Poran, M.A. (2006). The politics of protection: Body image, social pressures, and the misrepresentation of young Black women. *Sex Roles, 55*(11–12), 739–755.

Queen, C., & Comella, L. (2008). The necessary revolution: Sex-positive feminism in the post-Barnard era. *Communication Review, 11*(3), 274–291. doi:10.1080/10714420802306783.

Rae, I. (2016). The mis-adventures of awkward black girl [Internet Series]. http://awkwardblackgirl.com/.

Renold, E., and Ringrose, J. (2011). Schizoid subjectivities? Re-theorizing teen girls' sexual cultures in an era of 'sexualization'. *Journal of Sociology, 47*(4), 389–409.

Ringrose, J., & Renold, E. (2012). Slut-shaming, girl power, and 'sexualisation': Thinking through the politics of international SlutWalks with teen girls. *Gender & Education, 24*(3), 333–343.

Riskind, R.G., Tomello, S.L., Younger, B.C., & Patterson, C.J. (2014). Sexual identity, partner gender, and sexual health among adolescent girls in the United States. *American Journal of Public Health, 104*(10), 1957–1963.

Roberts, A., Cash, T.F., Feingold, A., & Johnson, B.T. (2006). Are black-white differences in females' body dissatisfaction decreasing? A meta-analytic review. *Journal of consulting and clinical psychology, 74*(6), 1121–1131. doi:http://dx. doi.org/10.1037/0022-006X.74.6.1121.

Romo, L., Kouyoumdjian, C., Nadeem, E., & Sigman, M. (2006). Promoting values of education in Latino mother-adolescent discussions about conflict and sexuality. In J. Denner & B. Guzmán (Eds.), *Latina girls: Voices of adolescent strength in the United States* (59–76). New York: NYU Press.

Roseboro, D. (2011). Hip hop, sexuality, and online magazines. In D. Carlson & D.L. Roseboro (Eds.), *The sexuality curriculum and youth culture* (328–347). New York: Peter Lang.

Ross, J.N., & Coleman, N.M. (2011). Gold digger or video girl: The salience of an emerging hip-hop sexual script. *Culture, Health & Sexuality, 13*(2), 157–171.

Sapphire. (1996). *Push.* New York: Alfred A. Knopf.

Saturday Night Live Writing Team & Michaels, L. (2016). The day Beyoncé turned black. In L. Michaels (Producer), *Saturday Night Live.* New York: NBC.

Schooler, D., Monique Ward, L., Merriwether, A., & Caruthers, A. (2004). Who's that girl: Television's role in the body image development of young white and black women. *Psychology of women quarterly, 28*(1), 38–47.

Scull, T.M., Malik, C.V., & Kupersmidt, J.B. (2014). A media literacy education approach to teaching adolescents comprehensive sexual health education. *Journal of Media Literacy Education, 6*(1), 1–14.

Sharpley-Whiting, T.D. (2007). *Pimps up, ho's down: Hip hop's hold on young black women.* New York: NYU Press.

Squires, C.R., Kohn-Wood, L.P., Chayous, T., & Carter, P.L. (2006). Evaluating agency and responsibility in gendered violence: African American youth talk about violence and hip hop. *Sex Roles, 55*, 725–737. doi:10.1007/s11199-006-9127-7.

Stephens, D., & Few, A. (2007). Hip hop honey or video ho: African American preadolescents' understanding of female sexual scripts in hip hop culture. *Sexuality & Culture, 11*(4), 48–69.

Stephens, D.P., & Phillips, L.D. (2003). Freaks, gold diggers, divas and dykes: The sociohistorical development of adolescent African American women's sexual scripts. *Sexuality & Culture, 11*, 3–49.

Stephens, D.P., & Phillips, L.D. (2005). Integrating Black feminist thought into conceptual frameworks of African American adolescent women's sexual scripting process. *Sexualities, Evolution and Gender, 7*, 37–55.

Stice, E. (2002). Risk and maintenance factors for eating pathology: A meta-analytic review. *Psychological Bulletin, 128*(5), 825–848.

Stice, E., Spangler, D., & Agras, W.S. (2001). Exposure to media-portrayed thin-ideal images adversely affects vulnerable girls: A longitudinal experiment. *Journal of Social and Clinical Psychology, 20*(3), 270–288.

Stokes, C.E. (2007). Representin' in cyberspace: Sexual scripts, self-definition, and hip hop culture in Black American adolescent girls' home pages. *Culture, Health & Sexuality, 9*(2), 169–184. doi:10.1080/13691050601017512.

Sussman, N.M., Truong, N., & Lim, J. (2007). Who experiences "America the beautiful"? Ethnicity moderating the effect of acculturation on body image and risks for eating disorders among immigrant women. *International Journal of Intercultural Relations, 31*(1), 29–49. doi:10.1016/j.ijintrel.2006.03.003.

Szymanski, D.M., Moffitt, L.B., & Carr, E.R. (2011). Sexual objectification of women: Advances to theory and research. *The Counseling Psychologist, 39*(1), 6–38.

Taylor, J., Gilligan, C., & Sullivan, A. (1995). *Between voice and silence: Women and girls, race and relationship.* Cambridge, MA: Harvard University Press.

Thomas, M. 2011. *Multicultural Girlhood: Racism, Sexuality and the Conflicted Spaces of American Education.* Philadelphia, PA: Temple University Press.

Thompson, M.S., & Keith, V.M. (2001). The blacker the berry: Gender, skin tone, self-esteem and self efficacy. *Gender and Society, 15*, 336–357.

Thompson, M.S., & Keith, V.M. (2004). Copper brown and blue black: In C. Herring, V. Keith, & H. D. Horton (Eds.) Colorism and self-evaluation. In *Skin deep: How race and complexion matter in the "color-blind" era* (pp. 45–64). Urbana, IL: University of Illinois at Chicago.

Tolman, D.L. (2012). Female adolescents, sexual empowerment and desire: A missing discourse of gender inequity. *Sex Roles, 66*(11–12), 746–757. doi:10.1007/s11199-012-0122-x.

Townsend, T.G., Thomas, A.J., Neilands, T.B., & Jackson, T.R. (2010). I'm no jezebel; I am young, gifted, and Black: Identity, sexuality, and Black girls.

Psychology of Women Quarterly, *34*, 273–285. doi:10.1111/j.1471-6402.2010.01574.x.

Trice, D.T. (2004, March 31). Morse Avenue harassment calls for action. *Chicago Tribune*. http://articles.chicagotribune.com/2004-03-31/news/0403310161_1_young-women-two-girls-boys.

Utsey, S., Giesbrecht, N., Hook, J., & Stanard, P. (2008). Cultural, sociofamilial, and psychological resources that inhibit psychological distress in African Americans exposed to stressful life events and race related stress. *Journal of Counseling Psychology*, *55*(1), 49–62.

Viladrich, A., Yeh, M.C., Bruning, N., & Weiss, R. (2009). "Do real women have curves?" Paradoxical body images among Latinas in New York City. *Journal of Immigrant and Minority Health*, *11*(1), 20–28.

Walker, A. (1983). *In search of our mother's gardens: Womanist prose*. San Diego, CA: Harcourt.

Walker, A. (1992). *The color purple*. London: Women's Press.

Wallace, S.A., Townsend, T.G., Glasgow, Y., & Ojie, M. (2011). Gold diggers, video vixens, and jezebels: Stereotype images and substance use among urban African American girls. *Journal of Women's Health*, *20*(9), 1315–1324. doi:10.1089/jwh.2010.2223.

Ward, M.L. (2004). Wading through the stereotypes: Positive and negative associations between media use and Black adolescents' conceptions of self. *Developmental Psychology*, *40*(2), 284–294.

Ward, L.M., Day, K.M., & Epstein, M. (2006). Uncommonly good: Exploring how mass media may be a positive influence on young women's sexual health and development. *New Directions for Child and Adolescent Research*, *112*, 57–70.

Ward, L.M., Hansbrough, E., & Walker, E. (2005). Contributions of music video exposure to black adolescents' gender and sexual schemas. *Journal of Adolescent Research*, *20*(2), 143–166.

Warren, C.S. (2014). Body area dissatisfaction in white, black and Latina female college students in the USA: An examination of racially salient appearance areas and ethnic identity. *Ethnic and Racial Studies*, *37*(3), 537–556.

Weekes, D. (2002). Get your freak on: How black girls sexualise identity. *Sex Education: Sexuality, Society and Learning*, *2*(3), 251–262.

West, C.M. (2009). Still on the auction block: The (s)exploitation of Black adolescent girls in rap(e) music and hip hop culture. In S. Olfman (Ed.), *The sexualization of childhood* (89–102). Westport, CT: Praeger Press.

Willoughby, V. (2016). Beyoncé's "Formation" is a celebration of unapologetic blackness. *Bitch Magazine*. https://bitchmedia.org/beyonce-formation-video-black-lives-matter-feminism-hearken.

Wingood, G.M. DiClemente, R.J., Bernhardt, J.M., Harrington, K., Davies, S.L., & Robillard, A. (2003). A prospective study of exposure to rap music videos and

African American female adolescents' health. *American Journal of Public Health*, *93*(3), 437–439.

Xie, B., Unger, J.B., Gallaher, P., Johnson, C.A., Wu, Q., Chou, C.P. (2010). Overweight body image, and depression in Asian and Hispanic adolescents. *American Journal of Health Behavior*, *34*(4), 476–488.

Young, J.A. (2008). Get in where you fit in: Hip-hop's muted voice on misogyny. California State University Northridge. http://www.csun.edu/~csbs/depart ments/pan_african_studies/pdf/get_in_where_you_fit_in.pdf.

Zavella, P. (2003). *Talkin' sex:* Chicanas and Mexicanas theorize about silences and sexual pleasure. In G.F. Arredondo, A. Hurtado, N. Klahn, O. Najera-Ramirez, & P. Zavella (Eds.), *Chicana feminisms: A critical reader*. Durham, NC: Duke University Press.

INDEX

© The Author(s) 2016   91
S. Lamb et al., *Girls of Color, Sexuality, and Sex Education*,
DOI 10.1057/978-1-137-60155-1